Don't Believe It!

DON'T BELIEVE IT!

How to Follow Your Dreams in
Spite of Those Who Say You Can't

Dan Montez

Whole Note Publishing

Don't Believe It!
How to Follow Your Dreams in Spite of Those Who Say You Can't
By Dan Montez

All rights reserved. No part of this book or its audio version may be reproduced or transmitted in any form or by any means, electronic or mechanical, including photocopying, recording, or by any information storage and retrieval system, without written permission from the author, except for the inclusion of brief quotations in a review.

This publication is designed to provide competent and reliable information regarding the subject matter covered. However, it is sold with the understanding that the author and publisher are not engaged in rendering legal, financial, or other professional advice. Readers assume all responsibility for their lives and decisions made as a result of reading or listening to (by audio version) the contents of this book. Laws and practices often vary from state to state and if legal or other expert assistance is required, the services of a professional should be sought. The author and publisher specifically disclaim any liability that is incurred from the use of application of the contents of this book.

Whole Note Publishing Edition
Copyright © 2007 by Dan Montez
All rights reserved.

All illustrations in this book Copyright © 2007 Tom Stigliano. Used by Permission. Illustrations may not be used for any purpose without express permission by the copyright owner.

Whole Note Publishing
service@danmontez.com
wholenote@optonline.net

ISBN print ed. 978-0-9801905-0-2
ISBN audio ed. 978-0-9801905-1-9

Contents

Introduction vii

Section I: The Dream Killers

1   The Ruthless Realists 1
2   The Pessimistic Pedagogues 7
3   The Frank Friends..13
4   The Critical Colleagues..19
5   The Concerned Kin 25
6   The Security Scarecrows 31
7   The Practiced Professionals 37
8   The Power Peddlers..43
9   The Muck Merchants 49

Section II: The Risk Taker

10 The Ask-for-What-You-Wanter........................57
11 The Unapproachables Approacher 63
12 The Approval Infringer...69
13 The Hoop Hater 75
14 The Fall-on-your-Facer...81
15 The Goal Setter...87
16 The Attitude Enhancer 93
17 The Solution Seeker..99
18 The Inner Voice Hearer 105
19 The Everybody Lover 111
20 The Faith Spreader 115

Introduction

It was like something out of the Twilight Zone. I looked around and found myself on a stage at Lincoln Center. There were thousands of people looking at me all at once from tiered seats and what seemed like endless balconies stretching into the heavens. In front of me was a huge orchestra with which I had never practiced. I was on a stage on which I had never rehearsed surrounded by a huge chorus I had never seen. We were all wearing makeup and I was in an extravagant costume I had never worn before. The lights were down on the audience and a spotlight was on me. The conductor looked at me and I knew that I

Don't Believe It!

was expected to start the opera with the first aria. I thought that I might wake up at any moment but realized that it was not a dream. I opened my mouth. Nothing came out. At one point someone in the cast must have noticed a glimmer of panic in my eye for he surreptitiously sidled up to me, in character, his back to the audience. With teeth clenched, he said, "Don't worry, they can hear you. The sound doesn't bounce back." Well, that's good to know, I thought.

During the aria, time seemed to stop and I was 18 again, singing the same song. I was at a university in the studio of the head of the voice department. I was thinking that, perhaps, I might want to be a voice major. After hearing me sing a few notes, he grabbed me by the arm and pushed me graciously out the door telling me that I had no voice, no business singing, and to please find something else to do. So I went to a different university in a different state. After trying to sing for the head of the opera department there, my arm was grabbed again, but this time he dragged me to the office of the head of another department, opened the door, shoved me in, and closed the door behind me.

Years later these two Doctors of Music would hear me again. One would be shocked to see me one evening as the lead tenor in a production of *Madama Butterfly*. And the other would approach me one day and apologize and say, "I never thought you had a beautiful voice."

Frankly, I didn't have a beautiful voice. In fact, it was quite frightful. But I did have one thing. I had a lively sense of "super independence."

I'm not sure when I became super independent. I think that perhaps it began when I was about three years old when my father left my mother. I think at

Introduction

that point, I stopped trusting authority figures in general. Not to say that that's good, but for me, it taught me to trust myself and ultimately to question the negativity of the world. I questioned everybody. I drove people nuts. When my mother remarried, I questioned my new father. I made people defend themselves and sometimes that got me in trouble. But most of the time, I ended up challenging the naysayers of the world. I especially enjoyed challenging people who said, "You can't."

You see, I believe that about 90% of the things we hear or see everyday are negative. We live in a world that focuses on problems and not solutions--in a world that specializes in collecting and propagating information on disasters and personal failures rather than successes and miracles. You cannot open a newspaper or turn on the evening news without being bombarded by negativity.

Some years ago, when my wife and I were the editors of a newsletter on positive attitudes, we spent week after week in the library sifting though newspapers and periodicals. We were specifically looking for positive stories. Some weeks, we couldn't find anything. However, on average, we would find maybe one article in every ten papers and it was buried on some inconsequential page. It seemed unbelievable to me. I asked myself, as I had throughout my life: How can we surround ourselves with all this without letting it affect our attitudes and expectations? I've always believed that you become what you surround yourself with. If you put trash in, you get trash out.

So, how do we deal with this? We can't hide in a closet and avoid the world. But we can believe in our dreams despite what everyone seems to be telling us. I

Don't Believe It!

have come to believe that to keep the garbage out, we must go on the offense. In this book, I am going to share with you two ways to prevail over pessimism and defeat the depressing drivel that encircles each of us daily. In the first section, you will learn to recognize and deal with negative people. In the second, you will learn to take risks and to step beyond the boundaries of what so-called "normal people" do. Am I saying you need to be abnormal? You bet! I don't believe that we live on earth to be normal or to "fit in," but rather to be unique and exceptional.

Section 1

The Dream Killers

Alas for those that never sing, but die with their music still in them.
    -Oliver Wendell Holmes

Chapter 1

The Ruthless Realists

What concerns me is not the way things are, but rather the way people think things are.
-Epictetus

Get ready to swim upstream. That's what you are going to have to do if you want to achieve your deepest desires. However, before we jump into the raging river together, we have to answer an important question. Here it is:

Don't Believe It!

What is real?

A nice, simple question. Actually, don't worry about completing your answer to this question before you start your journey. You'll start figuring it out along the way. But before you begin, it would help you to know a couple of things.

1. In spite of what every one tells you is real, you can achieve your dreams.
2. Reality will largely be how you choose to see it, hear it, and feel it.

Unfortunately, the word "real" has been forged into a tool to destroy dreams. You will often hear people say that you need to evaluate a situation more "realistically". Perhaps they will also try to define themselves with the label "realist." Here is the truth: People only use this word as an excuse to be negative.

Imagine a man standing on a sidewalk on a cold day in winter trying to sell ice cream. Another man approaches and they strike up a conversation. The first man says, "I don't seem to be selling a lot of ice cream today." The second man says, "Let's be realistic now. It's the middle of winter. People just don't buy ice cream when it's cold." Now who can imagine the second man responding instead with, "Let's be realistic now. People love ice cream. Business will pick up." It sounds a bit unusual, doesn't it? And yet, what can we learn from this about the way we view reality? Almost certainly, we should not use the word "realistic" in the second statement. We might use the word "positive" instead. Why? Because most of us see reality as bringing us from a more positive level to a more negative one. It's never the other way around.

The Ruthless Realists

What is reality? Perhaps another clue can be found in our subconscious. Under hypnosis, test volunteers are touched by a hypnotherapist's finger and told they are being touched by a hot poker. What is amazing, is that not only do they feel pain, but a blister actually rises on the skin. So what is real? Our senses tend to be the way we evaluate reality. As far as our senses are concerned, reality is what we most deeply believe.

When you are around negative people, you can tell that who they are greatly influences the things they see, hear and feel. One's expectations literally will filter out from the senses things that don't correspond with those expectations. Life becomes a reflection of our inner selves. We rarely notice anything that is not already part of what we are.

For example, you may have heard the story of the person who became extremely sick during a major football game. It was immediately attributed to some of the hot dogs being sold and so an announcement was made on the P.A. system. Within minutes, the first aid station was inundated with people throwing up and getting sick. However, it was later discovered that it was not the hot dogs at all, but rather a case of the flu the first person had contracted. People's belief that they could be sick, created a "real" physical response.

When people begin to create a new destiny, they see hear and feel what they want. In the business world today, people say they are changing their "paradigm" and becoming more "proactive" and not "reactive." They will choose a new way to interpret life that matches their dreams. If we choose to interpret life in our own way, is this somehow intellectually dishonest? Are we ignoring "reality"?

Don't Believe It!

Events are just events. Things are just things. If we want to know what is truly real, we need to be honest about that. Imagine that someone breaks into your house and steals your coat. Is this a "bad" or a "good" event? Is it a "happy" or a "sad" event? None of these; it is just an event. If you choose to feel like a victim, then you will have one answer. If, on the other hand, you think that maybe the man was starving and cold and needed the coat more than you, you will have another answer. Everything depends on perspective.

By choosing how to see, hear, or feel life, you are not being dishonest or ignoring reality. Rather, you are creating it. You are deciding that what you believe is real. Things are not "good" or "bad" but rather only how we use and interpret those things.

It is so important that you understand the concept of reality before you get very far into your journey. You will become bombarded by people who call themselves "realists." These self-described experts on reality have just simply chosen to see, hear and feel life more negatively than you have. Remember that.

I can't tell you how many times I have been asked when I was going to get a "real" job. However, every time that I'm asked the question, I remind myself that I must be doing something right. Learn to ask these people who call themselves "realists" to exactly define reality. They will always trap themselves into revealing who they are. Reality, to them will always be exactly how they see it and generally more negatively than how you see it.

If you want to succeed, you must realize that reality can be created. How many people never even tried to run a four-minute mile because they didn't believe that it could be done? How many aeronautical engineers didn't even try to break the sound barrier because they were taught that it was impossible? How many believed that humans would never reach the moon?

What do you believe is real? Your answer will either limit you or liberate you. As you make your way towards your dreams, learn to believe in your incredible potential. But, remember not to believe the Ruthless Realists, who tell you:

1. to look at life "realistically".
2. that things are constant and never change.
3. that you can't see life in your own way.
4. that your dreams are irrational.
5. that it can't be done.
6. that life is anything less than how you choose to see it, hear it and feel it. (However, keep an open mind if they tell you that it's something more!)
7. to get a "real" job.
8. not to buy ice cream in the winter.

Chapter 2

The Pessimistic Pedagogues

Ignorance of all things is an evil neither terrible nor excessive, nor yet the greatest of all; but great cleverness and much learning, if they be accompanied by a bad training, are a much greater misfortune.
-Plato

It wasn't long after I began school that I realized I thought differently from other kids. I was in the fourth grade and found myself in the office of the school psychologist being asked how many fingers she was holding up. I had failed an association test given to my class. The test was simple. The psychologist said a

Don't Believe It!

word and we were instructed to write down the first word that came to our mind. So, when she said apple, I, of course, thought of an orange. But I thought of "an orange"--the first word coming to mind being "an". So I filled my paper with "a"s, "an"s, and "the"s. I really wasn't trying to be a smart alec, I simply was taking the test in my own way. The school administrators never could understand why. I remember being extremely bored in class and never understanding why I needed to know what they were teaching me. So I spent classes driving a car across my desk or staring out of the window, daydreaming. The teacher immediately assumed that I was stupid and tried to hold me back a grade. Thanks to an assertive mother, I went on to fifth grade. There, after a class I.Q. test was given, I found myself brought out of the class again. This time instead of being asked how many fingers were being held up, I was being asked who I thought the next president should be and what I thought of world affairs.

Too often, teachers assume that if their message isn't getting across, that there must be something wrong with the student. Unfortunately these pedagogues spend their time trying to get information across without even attempting to sell the student on why he or she even needs (or wants) to know this information. "How does this apply to our lives?" "How will it help me?" It is a teacher's first duty to make sure the answers to these questions are clear in every student's mind.

I've never stopped asking teachers these questions. Unfortunately, I think it has aggravated most of them. One of my middle-school teachers, exasperated with my never-ending questions, suddenly bellowed during my history class, "Dan Montez, you are

The Pessimistic Pedagogues

a mental midget!" The name stuck, as my peers assigned me this wonderful nickname. My grades were never fabulous, especially when a teacher couldn't answer my questions. In eighth grade, I received my first (and only) "F" from my math and science teacher. Yet, at the end of the year when they gave the students a high school math placement exam, the teacher came to me in surprise when I received the highest grade in the school. He couldn't understand that even at this age, I had already developed a philosophy of education. I only cared about tests and grades when I wanted to care about them. And I only cared about what I wanted to know and when I wanted to know it. I felt knowledge should have application, learning should have direction and information should be coupled with values. Facts for the sake of facts seemed a self-indulgent waste of time. However, knowledge that could be used to make the world, and my life, better was more important.

Why the long discourse of my experiences? Because they are an example about the kinds of educational philosophies you are going to face as you gain knowledge that leads to your goals. So many teachers have ideas about knowledge that will be stumbling blocks for you as you follow your unique set of specific goals. In fact, most educators that I've come across prefer that you don't even have specific goals, so they can give you some goals that fit their curriculum. What you must keep in mind is that schools are there to serve the student--never the other way around.

In my experience, I haven't found a lot of happy teachers. There are the exceptions, but the maxim is too often true which says, "Those that can't do, teach." As a result, so many in the education profession look at life with a victim mentality. They also expect that since

Don't Believe It!

they had to become a teacher, so does everyone else. For example, in high school, I began my real love affair with classical music. But most of my teachers and counselors told me not to get too serious about it. They told me that I couldn't make money in this profession, that it was a waste of time, that no one ever makes it, or that there is just too much competition. I was assaulted at every front with negativism.

This continued through college. Even the teachers that handed out music performance degrees told me to get my degree in education and get a credential so I would "have something to fall back upon." One singing professor actually told me, "There are only two things you can do with your singing degree: Sing opera or teach. It's too hard to do the first and so you better count on the second."

It's so easy for students to believe the faithless negativity of their teachers. After all, we entrust these people with our minds and our children's minds. Over half of most of our early life is spent in school. Most children spend more time with their teachers than with their own parents. We teach our children to respect their teachers because information is power in today's world. There is something holy about the way we treat the knowledge industry. However, when we start doing graduate work, the holy walls of truth and pure information begin to break down. All of the knowledge we thought was absolute as an undergraduate becomes suspect. We can take almost any side of any issue, defend it, and footnote it. Doctors begin quoting one another. In the end, he who has the longest bibliography wins.

The purpose of most educational systems today is not to arrive at truth. Instead it is to question the existence of any truths. In fact, the systems exist often to simply maintain the life of the systems. That's fine, except most teachers hide this fact until you get to graduate school. Once there you learn only to create greater questions. The more you learn, the less you realize you know. The truly enlightened scholar ends up not really knowing anything, but being as opinionated as he can be. Unfortunately, many young minds (and many old minds) don't understand this and think the teacher is a repository of truth. Some teachers even want their students to believe this. Don't!

Instead, allow them to help you, but don't allow them to attack your dreams. If they have more knowledge than you, it's just because they've studied more. It doesn't mean they are right. Rest assured that there is someone just as smart as they are who disagrees with them. Teachers can too often destroy a student's aspirations with a single glance. If you hold your teacher's beliefs in higher esteem than your own, that glance will kill you.

When I was doing my graduate work, I came up with an idea to study a branch of music that was rarely studied. I was very excited that I had found a practically untouched area of vocal music my professors knew nothing about. My idea was attacked immediately. But I soon received a grant from an outside source to continue my research in Europe. This of course shocked my professors. After a year of hard work, I sang some of this rare music for the first time in the United States. As a result, the concert was recorded with an interview on National Public Radio's (NPR), Performance Today. Although perhaps it was not completely true, they hailed me on the air as the nation's expert on the subject. Immediately I was

Don't Believe It!

approached by a professor at the university who said, "If what you were doing was so important and such a new idea, someone would have thought about it before. Anyway, I'm going to be on NPR too!" Of course I should have thought that I couldn't possibly have an original idea! Interestingly enough, my first CD to hit record stores happened to be of this music, because no one had thought of it.

In summary, don't believe the Pessimistic Pedagogues who:

1. say you can't.
2. put down your dreams as unimportant.
3. haven't achieved their own dreams.
4. seem unhappy.
5. grimace when asked a question.
6. act like you are their competition.
7. tell you to study something to "fall back upon."
8. tell you what you want or need to know but don't tell you why.
9. ask you how many fingers they are holding up.

Chapter 3

The Frank Friends

Most people enjoy the inferiority of their best friends.
-Lord Phillip Chesterfield

One of my better teachers in high school introduced me to the phrase, " With friends like that, who needs enemies?" When I first heard this, it didn't seem to make any sense. Why would people choose to have friends that were nasty or mean? It's still positively amazing to me the kind of friends some people will attract to themselves.

Some people are like powerful magnets,

attracting unbelievable abuse into their lives. How many times have you seen someone in an abusive relationship finally get out, only to get into another one just as bad or worse? I don't believe these things are coincidences. I believe that we attract people into our lives that correspond to our own self-images. We attract who we think we deserve as friends and mates.

This chapter is not meant to teach you how to get out of abusive relationships. There are many more thorough treatments of the subject. But because our self-images are not perfect, we need to be aware that we may now be in negative relationships. We need to be alerted to the things we may attract into our lives through our own negative thoughts.

Another thing we attract into our lives is our fears. This is because we attract everything we dwell on. Too often we focus on what we don't want at the expense of focusing our minds on what we do want. For example, people frequently pray for a negative. Many will pray, "Please, God, don't let me be fat" or "Help me stop smoking and drinking." But what do they want?! How about, "Please, God, let me look like a million bucks" or " Help me to be healthy!"

Surrounding yourself with good things and good people is largely a matter of focus. However, since most of us are in a process of self-image building, we may have attracted some people to our lives that don't want to allow us to grow. In fact, we may not even be aware that we have friends like this.

Because we call them friends, we often open ourselves up to subtle attacks on our self-images and our dreams. This is not to say that we shouldn't have friends, or that we start interpreting the things that our friends say in the worst possible ways. But, try to watch out for a few things.

The Frank Friends

We turned on the television at our home one evening and the cartoon "The Simpsons" was on. Homer had his arm around his son Bart in an intimate father-son talk. He said, "Sometimes the only way to feel good about yourself is to make someone else feel bad." We laugh, but often our very friends will put us down because they feel so poorly about themselves.

That show reminded me of the only time I ever punched somebody in the nose. I was in the fifth grade and was far from being the physically aggressive type. I wasn't very popular, but one of the boys, who also wasn't very popular, decided to start pushing me around. He thought that I might be an easy way to gain popularity. I was going to be the tool of his aggrandizement. He grabbed my sweater and started yelling at me for no reason except to attract attention to himself from the other boys. I told him to let go of my sweater, which just made him yank on it more and try to rip it. It seemed that the only way to protect my sweater (and my pride) was to haul off and bop him one. No sooner had I done so, when I suddenly became the popular one among the other boys.

We have to watch the kinds of friends we make and also watch the way we make them. Many of those who claim to be our friends only like us when we aren't accomplishing anything. As soon as we start to follow our goals, they begin to feel guilty about their own lives. At this point, a number of things can happen. They may try to put down your dreams or minimize their importance. Or they may simply try to make you feel guilty for your accomplishments through accusations of conceit. They may actually try to make you think that you are the one separating yourself from them because of your selfish ideas of grandeur.

Don't Believe It!

When things get really bad, your worst friends start asking that question we talked about before, "When are you going to get a 'real' job?" This happens because most people who follow their dreams work for themselves. Actually, everyone who follows their dreams works for themselves. Even the employed treat the business as if it were their own. But of course, no one should enjoy their job! Then it wouldn't be a "real" job. This is especially true when our friends have a "real" job.

Often, many give up the pursuit of their dream because they are subconsciously afraid of losing their friends. However, friends who keep you from your dreams are not your friends. Often, those who begin to find success need to make new friends. But the next time around, they find true friends. They find others who support their dreams, who believe in setting goals, and who understand the difficulties of attainment. Generally, this is because they have walked the path themselves.

It's important to remember the negative things your friends tell you along the path when you do succeed. It will strengthen your faith in future goals at a time when the negative attacks will start coming on a higher, more intense level.

I remember one of my friends from church. When I was about fifteen, she approached me one Sunday and told me that I would never amount to anything as a musician and was wasting my time in what I was trying to do. I immediately told her, with a smile on my face, that she would someday see my name in lights. She laughed and derided me for my vain and foolish ideas. She said that it would never happen. Her words stuck with me during all of my struggles, and I used them as one of my motivators to achieve my dream. When lights surrounded my name at Carnegie Hall, I took pictures and remembered my childhood friend. Although she hadn't seen me for about two decades, in my heart I thanked her for leading me to my dream.

To recap, don't believe the Frank Friends who:

1. use you to make themselves feel better.
2. put you down.
3. make fun of your dreams.
4. ask you when you are going to stop enjoying your work.
5. use friendship as an excuse to criticize you.
6. stop liking you because you are successful.
7. pull your sweater.

Chapter 4

The Critical Colleagues

*To avoid criticism,
do nothing,
say nothing,
be nothing.*
            -Elbert Hubbard

In just about every profession there are other people on similar paths to your own. You may have to work with them and even see them every day. Among these colleagues, some have dreams and some do not. Everyone is on a different path. Some want great success, others are there only to taste the profession,

Don't Believe It!

and still others are trying to prove to themselves that their efforts will fail. To this last group, life is a crapshoot and their dreams are pure torture. Nevertheless, many of them enjoy telling you how to improve your performance or change your life.

In general, co-workers who criticize your performance without being asked to cannot be trusted with your dreams. You should always listen to and consider criticism from all sources if you want to grow. However, valid or not, all criticism comes as a result of the motivations of the person offering it. It is important not only to question the criticism, but also the motivations. This is because the temptation will come to share and discuss your path and goals with people who have very negative agendas. Those who offer unsolicited criticism usually do so because they feel powerless themselves in some area of their lives. As a result, they try to exert control over others. People who are comfortable with themselves generally are more concerned with their own self-improvement and don't have time to save the world.

Another kind of colleague may feel just as insecure, but instinctively knows that it is not safe to criticize others to their faces. So they spend time gossiping about their colleagues behind their backs. I cannot emphasize this enough: Do not indulge in conversations with colleagues that put down anyone else in your profession. This is a great temptation. But rest assured that, when you're not present, they are gossiping about you. Anyone who will talk to you about someone else, will talk to someone else about you. Always.

I was away singing an opera, and between rehearsals, the cast went out to dinner together. Half way through our repast, one of my colleagues piped up and said that we were all prostitutes. Asked what he meant, he explained that we were willing to say, do, and sing anything anyone wanted for money. He complained that we couldn't create real art, but that we were willing to compromise ourselves to get a job. His victim mentality seemed appealing to the other singers who mostly simply nodded their heads in robotic agreement. I vocally disagreed with him and told him that for me, if I chose to accept a job, it was my choice. I affirmed that I was not a victim of others but that my life was a direct result of the choices I have made. He became very angry as he attempted to defend his helplessness. While watching his work in rehearsals, I noticed indeed that he would say and do anything to please his employers. He would often tell them how much he loved their ideas and would act like their best friends. Then immediately after rehearsals, he would bad-mouth these same people and criticize the very ideas he claimed he loved. There was no misunderstanding. He was acting out his negative worldview and getting exactly what he most deeply believed. He was living a double life, believing one thing and doing another--a sure recipe for unhappiness.

The smartest of the insecure colleagues are the ones that don't criticize you or your colleagues because they know that "what goes around, comes around." So instead, they do something absolutely ridiculous and detrimental to their own careers. They gossip about those at the top of their profession, with whom they have no dealings.

Nowhere does this seem to be more prevalent than at the university level. Here, students feel that in order to have a critical mind, they must tear apart those who are the most successful.

Don't Believe It!

I recall, when at the university, being involved with many other aspiring singers. Every semester there was a new group of colleagues, many involved in opera workshops, or actual productions. It was difficult, if not impossible, to hold a conversation about singing without the conversation taking a negative turn. Generally, this would be in the form of criticism of colleagues not present, or, more particularly, what's wrong with Pavarotti, Domingo, or some other famous singer. The students seemed to receive great joy from this process as if somehow, this criticism put them above these great singers.

When I got a part-time job singing in a restaurant, it got even worse. The other singers would eat dinner between sets and do nothing for the hour except bad-mouth famous singers. Interestingly enough, some of these other singers had been singing in that restaurant for more than ten years. That's it. That was their career. None of them has made it even close to the level of the people they criticized.

These colleagues at the university and restaurant seemed to think that they were safe from reproach for this kind of talk. However they missed a couple of important points.

First, their focus was negative. They would do so much better to focus on what these great singers (including their colleagues) do well. I'll say it again: Focusing on what we want, not on what we don't want, brings success.

Second, they were sabotaging themselves. The way they criticize another performer on the stage will be exactly the way they expect their audience to judge them when they are on stage. Try performing for people that you think hate you or do not have your best interests at heart. No wonder there is so much stage

The Critical Colleagues

fright! When you sit in an audience and support, love and want the best for your co-workers, you will be calm and not fear your audience. Here's a little Zen: You are them and they are you. This goes for every profession, for we are all on the stage of life and have to take our turn. Fear is the greatest crippler in this society.

Did these critics ever wonder why Pavarotti and Domingo are where they are today? They must have done something that these critics haven't done. Don't fall into the trap of believing that those at the top of your profession got where they are because they paid somebody off, slept with someone, or somehow cheated. These stories make good novels or T.V. movies, but they are not the norm. Once you start believing these things, you will automatically believe that you are not in control of your own destiny, but rather a victim of unkind fate. Subsequently, your belief will create the fact. Then you can run around saying, "I told you so" and pass your negativity to the next generation.

Finally, when a colleague succeeds where you have not, even if you feel you have superior talent and ability, be happy for them. Only wish the best upon others, and the world will wish its best on you.

To whom do we listen if not our critical colleagues? Get advice only from people who have already done exactly what you want to do. If you want a million dollars, don't ask a financial planner who doesn't have a million dollars to tell you how to do it. If you want to sing for a living, only take advice from someone who has succeeded in doing so. Advice should generally come from above and not the side. You get the picture.

Here are the rules. Don't believe the Critical

Don't Believe It!

Colleagues who:

1. put down other associates.
2. are negative about the prospects of their profession.
3. criticize those at the top of their profession.
4. constantly give you unsolicited criticism.
5. haven't achieved success themselves yet.
6. call themselves prostitutes.
7. sing at restaurants.

Chapter 5

The Concerned Kin

Most people are other people. Their thoughts are someone else's opinions, their lives a mimicry, their passions a quotation.
— *Oscar Wilde*

When I was six years old, I went kite flying with my family. The time came that I needed to visit the bathroom, so I went in with my kite. When I came out, my family began laughing hysterically. I looked down and noticed that my kite string had gotten caught in my zipper. I tried to liberate the string, but it was

Don't Believe It!

hopelessly entangled. The more I tried, the harder my family laughed. I was quite embarrassed. Since then, I have tried to stop flying kites in the restroom. However, through the years, my family has brought the event up from time to time to embarrass me. We allow our families to do things like this because we love them. We let them laugh at, point out, and even give advice about our mistakes.

Of course, as we mature and grow in different directions, our opinions about what is a mistake and what is not may begin to differ. However, the openness remains. At this point, we need to be sure not to confuse the love we feel for our family with the advice they are giving. This especially applies when it concerns our dreams.

When I first decided to major in music, I believe my family was a bit nonplussed. No one had been a professional musician in our family for as many generations as we knew. My stepfather came to me and wanted to know if I would like to be a partner in his business when he retired. I imagined the words "and Son" added to the sign on the front of his independent insurance agency. As moved as I was by this, I knew it didn't fit into my plans.

If I hadn't really known what I wanted, my father's love could have confused me. But instead, I told him what I wanted to do and he graciously backed away.

By my senior year at the university, when I abruptly decided to become an opera singer, I know I shocked my family. I know they really didn't like classical music to begin with, and opera?! It was difficult to get any member of my family to attend my first performances as a singer. I know that it wasn't because they didn't love me, but I know when they weighed making me feel good against the long drive to hear a fat lady screaming, the fat lady tipped the scales. Later, however, they began to see me periodically, and my dad actually cried once. (Puccini does that to even the strongest constitutions.)

Over the years, I've made a lot of mistakes with my family as well. About a year after getting married, we moved in with my parents for a few months. (Stop laughing.) I seriously don't advise this. Nothing will encourage advice giving more than acting dependent again. Please remember this. Every time you ask for help, be ready for criticism. Every time you whine or act helpless in front of others, others will feel they have permission to "fix" you. There's nothing wrong with asking for help, just be ready for "extra" help.

Secondly, don't make the mistake of discussing money with your family if you can avoid it. People are weird about money. Just wait for someone to pass away in your family and watch the madness happen. People you think you've known your whole life turn out to be very different than you had thought. If you are having money problems, and tell them, get ready for some strong opinions about your life. When you get yourself into tough situations, and your family starts helping, you begin feeling guilty obligations to follow their advice. This is fine if the advice is good. However, if it's not supportive of your dreams, you may find yourself in a nasty situation. So, talk at your own risk.

If you get married to a loving, supportive spouse, as I did, don't think that the advice will stop with him or her. Now, you have in-laws to deal with. Like it or not, they have become your second family. These people, who were originally strangers, now rise to the level of openness previously allowed only in your own

Don't Believe It!

family. What's worse, they're not prepared for you like your family is. As a result, there may be some rocky roads as they get to know both you and your aspirations.

Not long after my wife and I were married, we started making decisions on how we wanted to grow and what we wanted to do. One day we made a decision that my in-laws strongly disagreed with. They naturally voiced their opposition with my wife in no uncertain terms. She was torn. Should she please her parents whom she had known her whole life, or please her husband whom she had known for a year? Then I did a foolish thing, and let my pride get in the way. I wrote her parents a terse letter that I have regretted sending to this day. I hadn't yet realized that I had adopted, through marriage, another set of opinions about life.

Unlike the other kinds of people who criticize your aspirations, families are unique. You want to maintain a special kind of loving relationship not necessary to any of the other categories discussed in this book. So, when you decide to reject any kind of negativity, be careful.

If you don't follow your family's advice, they may take it as a personal rejection. All you can often do is tell them that you truly love them. Let them know that this love would be impossible if you didn't love yourself first by following your dreams. They need to be told that if you acquiesced to their emotional demands, you couldn't be doing so out of love as they suggest, but out of guilt.

This may seem difficult to understand, let alone explain to your Critical Kin, but it is worth the trouble to try. This book is about your dreams and following the path that will bring you the most joy. Just because we happen to be surrounded by negative people doesn't mean our lives need to be unhappy. Happiness and joy come from within and should not be dependent on external events or people.

One thing I want you to understand: when I speak of loving yourself first in order to love others, I am not speaking about selfishness. I am not speaking about sacrificing your relationships for your dreams. I believe that family relationships are the most important relationships we can have. They teach us love, service and the good kinds of sacrifice that make life worth living. Growing together with others in a loving relationship is the best and fastest way to grow as a person. In today's selfish society, this idea is becoming very unpopular. But it is not a sign of weakness to tell you that I know that without my wife, my dreams would be hollow. Dreams are more meaningful, exciting and joyful when shared with someone you love. You learn to move together in support of one another. It can be WIN-WIN! To be so single-minded toward a goal as to sacrifice this kind of growth opportunity is the epitome of selfishness, emptiness and loneliness. Life is not about giving one up for the other, but about balance. So, although you should reject giving up your dreams for your kin, you should equally reject giving up your most important relationships for your lust for wealth, power, or fame. Keep all your noble dreams.

In summary, when dealing with family members, don't believe them when they:

1. are embarrassed by your dreams.
2. use being a member of the family as an excuse to put down your dreams.
3. don't want to understand your dreams.

Don't Believe It!

4. don't seem to support you. They probably still love you.
5. never followed their own dreams.
6. are intimidated by you.
7. accuse you of thinking you are becoming "too good for the rest of us".
8. laugh at you when you get your kite string stuck in your zipper.

Chapter 6

The Security Scarecrows

Fear is proof of a degenerate mind.
-Virgil

Just as you start down the path toward your goals, offers like the one my father offered me will start knocking at your door. As you get closer to your goal, even more compelling alternatives will present themselves, offering you security and stability. Voices will sound in your ears that may say, "This opportunity will not come again," or, "Get out while you still can!"

Don't Believe It!

The voices may come from people, or from inside your head after years of security brainwashing as you grew up in society.

For example, it may have begun for you when you received your first "allowance" from your parents. I remember getting my first allowance and thinking about how exciting it was to start getting money from this seemingly magical source. I never really stopped to think, as a child, where my dad had gotten it. But I remember that after some time had passed, I started thinking that I deserved it. It came on the same day every week, and I expected it. Then one day, the magic broke. My father went through some rough times financially and the allowance stopped. Once again, I realized that security in life was a little unstable. (I didn't even have a clue as to how unstable.)

Interestingly enough, people tend to be obsessed with finding security. They would rather be secure than ever accomplish anything important with their lives. As they get older, society teaches them how to maintain the status quo and live risk-free. It does this in a number of ways.

One way is that our society tells us that we need a formal education to become successful. Don't get me wrong! I firmly believe in educating oneself. The more we know about the world, the better we communicate. The more we know about our chosen path, the better we will do. Information is great, but creation is better. Unfortunately, most university training these days is used as a security blanket for our failure to create anything. You see, there are those that do, and those that create. Those that know how to use a computer and those that invent the computer. Those who invent the light bulb and those that know how to turn on the bathroom light. Schools generally teach you to labor for someone else's dream and very little about how to create your own. It is true that some innovative programs are being implemented, but I have yet to see a school require a class on goal setting or having a positive attitude. In addition, it would be wonderful to see a scholarly institution put half of its curriculum behind the so-called "creative half" of their students' brains. Why did Einstein play the violin? For ideas! To gain access to the creative. Why are there so many successful people in the world without college degrees?

    I had the great opportunity to be directed by the famous opera singer and music theater performer Giorgio Tozzi. The majority of the world knows him from his performance in the movie, *South Pacific*, and his acclaimed recordings and performances on Broadway and at the Met. After a rehearsal one day, during a conversation, he told me that he hadn't even received a bachelor's degree. I was a bit surprised, considering not only what he knew, but that he had retired to teach in one of the most famous music schools in the U.S. Then he explained that he had accumulated enough university credit hours for a Doctorate, but simply didn't have the time nor feel it necessary to pursue it formally. What an important lesson! He went to college to learn what he wanted. It was his tool. He was not the tool of any university in doing what would serve it best. He created his own security by learning what would make him the best at what he did.

    Aside from society's love affair with education, it also is enamored with the insurance industry. This is direct security you can pay for on the spot. Although both my stepfather and father-in-law own insurance

Don't Believe It!

agencies, I have some reservations about the business. Many are already concerned about the economic effects of the industry and how costs are passed on to the consumer. However, we should be even more concerned about how the fear of disaster can affect our expectations and subsequently result in attracting the very thing we are buying the insurance for. But, this doesn't seem to concern most people because the majority of people in our society lead fear-based lives. As a result, the hunger for security intensifies.

When we start to involve ourselves in the unorthodox practice of dreaming, people will seemingly come out of the woodwork to tell you to find something to "fall back upon." In an effort to care about the weakest among us, government often creates things to save us when things fall apart. Although this can be a good thing, it can also be bad for us. Because we know that the security blanket is there, we may not try to lift ourselves out of our own problems. In fact, some people will begin to see this safety net as a "right" and abdicate their own responsibilities to themselves. I believe in helping the helpless. We are all beggars to some degree. However, I also believe that we must work as if it is all up to us and ignore the existence of safety nets. We can create them for others, but we must not create them for ourselves. Generally, when we create something to "fall back" upon, we "fall back" upon it! If we don't create it for ourselves then we are forced to achieve our dreams. We can burn some of the bridges that lead to havens of security that keep us from becoming exceptional human beings.

Taking responsibility for everything that happens to us in our lives is key. Stop playing the blame game. We are exactly where we are because of choices we have made up to this point. Do bad things happen to good people? Sure! Does blaming help? Never. You can learn, you can change things, and you can make new decisions. You can choose to feel like a victim and demand your rights, or you can choose to feel powerful and take responsibility. This means that you can choose how to "respond." Stop focusing on your rights more than you focus on your responsibilities. Stop being afraid.

Stop believing the Security Scarecrows that tell you:

1. that you must have something to "fall back on."
2. you'll never get a good job without a diploma.
3. you must work for someone else.
4. you can avoid pain.
5. you can avoid creativity.
6. you can avoid hard work.
7. you are going to get an allowance.

Chapter 7

The Practiced Professionals

Power is not sufficient evidence of truth.
-Samuel Johnson

For a moment, imagine the person or persons you admire most in your dream profession. It may be somebody that you idolize, who is doing what you would like to do, or whose opinion you trust most. Now, imagine yourself meeting this person. You show him what you can do and share your private dreams

Don't Believe It!

with him. But then, all of a sudden, he tells you that you are wasting your time. He doesn't like what you do, or he tells you that you don't have what it takes to achieve your dreams.

This type of person is worse than any of the other negative people we have discussed so far. This is because he has achieved your dream! He himself knows what it takes to do what you want and he knows what it's like to have a dream and work for it. Nothing can be more devastating that having a Practiced Professional trample upon your dreams. And yet...

Don't believe it!

If you can be rejected by the people you idolize and trust most, you can make it! You see, as you begin your climb to your goal, you will be rejected many times by people in your field who are much further up the ladder than you. Does this mean that you shouldn't have idols? Not necessarily. But what it means is that you shouldn't idolize any entire person; rather you should admire certain aspects. You should never idolize someone to the degree that you give him the power to destroy your dreams.

I thought it was unlikely that one of the greats that I respected and trusted in my field would personally attack and reject me. But I was wrong. After hearing me sing one evening, the bomb came. In fact not only did this person reject me, but it was in front of most of my colleagues. We're not talking about simple criticism here, but an absolute rejection of my work. I thought for a moment that I wanted to die or crawl into a hole when the eyes of all my colleagues all turned upon me in stunned silence.

Luckily, my "question authority figures"

mechanism kicked in just in time to keep me from abandoning my career before I had barely begun. In addition, this experience became a defining and liberating one for me. The last person on earth that I thought had the power to discourage me from my goals had failed to do so! I was free! Be ready for a similar moment. We are all tested before we succeed--some of us many times over. Each of us has to face our biggest fears before we accomplish our deepest desires.

One would think that these professionals would know better and remember what they went through. But, guess what--they are human too. Some just say things without thinking. Others, however, may have very negative agendas. They feel that the only way they can continue to feel unique and special is to make sure that what they do never becomes commonplace.

I was appearing on a television show with another professional opera singer and we were being interviewed. Half way through the program we were asked how we became singers and how a person becomes a singer. I immediately expressed my firm conviction that a singing voice, as well as a performing career, can be built. I asserted that it took hard work, dedication, and a belief in one's ability to overcome obstacles. What was intended to be a friendly, promotional program for an upcoming performance became a philosophy contest. The other singer immediately shot back that she disagreed with me and that "you either have it or you don't." She expressed that she believed that one is born "that way" and that there are some things that "can't be taught." I'm sure her philosophy brought her some sort of comfort. However, these clichés are killing the spirit of those struggling to achieve their dreams. So many of them

Don't Believe It!

are filled with self-doubt to begin with, unsure that they were one of the lucky ones to be "born that way." Usually, all that keeps them going is a fragile thread of faith. In my own darkest times, the only thing keeping me going was the belief that I could learn how to sing and act if I worked hard enough. I learned that sometimes one has to take a few steps into the darkness before they see the light.

When we are learning a new skill for the first time, we need to learn from all the sources that we can. But, that doesn't mean we should get into the habit of blindly believing anything a professional says just because they have more knowledge and experience. Knowledge and experience are a good reason to listen, but not to believe.

When I was studying piano, I recall asking my piano teacher once why I needed to express the Beethoven Sonata I was playing in a certain way. Tired of my endless questions, she blew up at me and said, "I'm a third generation Beethoven!" She then quoted me her educational pedigree back to Beethoven. She concluded by telling me to shut up, not question, and that if I didn't believe her, to find another teacher. So, I shut up for the day, but I never forgot the experience. It was an important lesson to me about how professionals, when probed too deeply, can resort to intimidation to maintain their power base.

Another kind of intimidation is the idea that there is "nothing new under the sun." If you are climbing up a ladder no one has climbed before, you especially need to watch out for sniper attacks from those who have climbed ladders next to yours. People who have excelled in a related category can get downright vicious if you are trying to break new ground.

The Practiced Professionals

A movie I highly recommend, *Strictly Ballroom*, has a defining moment for the Practiced Professionals in the dance world. They make an official announcement that there are "no new steps." In secret chambers the judges of the competition assert that if they don't know a step, they can't teach it. And if they can't teach it, they are all out of a job. As soon as you try something new in your field you will be jeopardizing the careers of others. In my field, the first tenor to hit a full chest "high C" was Duprez in Paris. The audiences were so astounded, that they didn't want to hear anyone else sing. The house tenor at the time, who couldn't do it, was so distraught, that he finally threw himself out of a window in 1839 and killed himself. Sounds like an opera, doesn't it? And yet today, practically all tenors are expected to hit high "C"s.

In American history, some wanted to close the U.S. Patent office, because they thought that everything that could be invented had been invented. The truth is, is that there will always be new human accomplishments, new ladders to climb, and new steps to learn.

Metropolitan opera star, Irene Dalis, once told me, "In this business, honey, you have to have the skin of an elephant and the heart of a butterfly."

In other words, keep your sensitivity, but never believe the Practiced Professionals that tell you:

1. you're not cut out for your chosen profession.
2. you're not talented enough to learn.
3. based on their "professional opinion," you can't make it.
4. you need to conform to what the rest of the "professional world" does.

Don't Believe It!

5. you have to accept what they say because of their credentials.
6. there are no "new steps."
7. they are related to Beethoven.

Chapter 8

The Power Peddlers

*Insects sting, not from malice, but because they want to
live. It is the same with critics—
they desire our blood, not our pain.*
                    -Nietzsche

A s you begin to be recognized for what you do, you will start meeting a new group of people. Just when you think that you are beginning to control your own destiny, they show up and tempt you to believe that you are not. This group includes a number of people including those with control over money, those

Don't Believe It!

who own or run the business you must deal with, agents, and professional critics. They are all in a constant wrestle for power. Power is their game. As soon as you start doing something important, they will find you and try to use you to make money.

Upon finishing my university studies, I was contacted by my first New York agent. She had heard me sing in Nevada and wanted to represent me. I was very naive and tried to be friendly and open with her about my ambitions. During a phone call to her one day, she just cut me off and said, "Listen, you are nothing but a piece of meat. We see you. We use you. We make a profit off of you. You are only a number. I don't want to know how you feel about anything. If I can sell you, that's all that matters." I was so appalled, I terminated our relationship. What an eye opener!

As I began getting jobs, I realized what meat felt like. Opera houses that booked me through agents were also after money (especially if they called themselves "non-profit"). They have different decisions to make. They will often hire an inferior singer because the singer has a better publicist or because that singer receives support from an important donor of the company. At one opera house where I performed, the leading lady was married to the conductor and at another the soprano was having an affair with the General Manager.

I know that I mentioned earlier that you should never assume that people get jobs in the ways we are discussing. That's still true. I am trying to point out that you will have experiences that will try to tempt you to believe you are not in control. These temptations will come in moments of self-doubt. The truth is that although these things happen, they are not the norm. Be prepared for these things and take them with a grain of salt. They are not as significant as your negative acquaintances would like you to believe.

There are more. Another thing companies will do to try to save money is to sacrifice the creative integrity of an opera by cutting pieces out of it. This keeps them from having to pay a union orchestra and union chorus overtime for longer works. My debut at Lincoln Center was so abrupt for this very type of reason. No stage time, no time with the chorus, no orchestra, no costume, no dress rehearsal. It all costs too much and there are a hundred other tenors standing in line behind you who would love to take your place. Because of the state of unions and the struggle for money, an interesting thing happens. Being the only traveling performers with the company, the stars will often be receiving a tenth the salary of the chorus person they are standing next to on stage. There are only exceptions for the really big names in the business. After dealing with these situations for a while, one might get discouraged or tempted to believe that you are simply a piece of meat and not a human being. But it's not over yet.

As you begin to share your gifts with the public, your work will be evaluated. In my business, it's by newspaper critics. They are often referred to in the business as a "necessary evil." Companies use them to promote their business and quote them in their advertising. For some strange reason, the public seems to think that because an opinion appears in the paper, it should hold more weight. As a result, companies and performers have come to depend on them for their own advertising. The evil comes because if you want them to say something good about you, you've got to run the risk that they will say something bad. I'm not sure

Don't Believe It!

why. Many of them seem to take great joy in trying to make or break careers. Unfortunately, there are no critics for critics, so they can say just about anything they want. Most of them have never done what we do, nor do they understand the inside process as well as they think they do. There is no science to it. All you have to do is watch Ebert and Roeper to know that even the best of them cannot agree when they see the same thing. It's important to remember that nobody has ever erected a statue to a critic. So why do we have them? Do they really think that their opinion will improve the quality of the performance?

I remember being reviewed in my first Italian opera. One newspaper loved me and said that I was perfect for the part, while another said I should have called upon my understudy. It can be tough on you when you put so much work into a project and the next day hundreds of thousands of people in the city read that you are the biggest failure in the universe. The most popular critical writing style often hurts those with even the thickest of skins and one might describe it as legalized libel. Although this will never happen, I am of the opinion that so-called critics would do a greater service for mankind if they focused on the positive aspects of what they are evaluating and relaxed a bit with the negative. If they don't like something, they should keep it to themselves. I can hear them laughing now. Oh well, I thought I would try.

The point is that when you start going after your dreams, watch out for these professional gossipmongers who will evaluate your work. Many will hate it and do their best to let the world know. If they are right about their criticism, then change and grow. If they are wrong, then don't believe it. You should learn to accept truth from any source—even critics!

However, what you know about your own performance is much more important than anything anyone else thinks. You must also remember that if you believe the good reviews, you must also believe the bad ones. Always listen, but ultimately make your own decisions. Don't allow your dreams to be destroyed by any critic.

The last kind of power broker you will have to deal with are the ones with the money. They can throw great sums around to get what they want. They can give money to an opera company and coyly request them to hire their favorite singer. They will give large sums of cash to a major record label to produce a recording with their favorite singer, while hiring already famous singers to sing along side. You might call this fame through association. Sometimes, they find ways to give the money directly to the singer and write it off their taxes. Sometimes singers will go to competitions and see the politics involved or they will try to get a job and find they are too good. For example, the supporters of major names in the business will often pressure the company to hire singers that are slightly inferior to the one they support so that their singer looks good. The illusions of marketing seem to run everything.

And this is just my profession. There are parallels in every job. Have I scared you to death? It may seem that what I am saying is that the best are not always chosen, that no matter how hard you work, something will thwart you. I am not saying that. I just don't want you to be surprised about how nasty things might get. Can we fight these powerful forces? Absolutely. Don't be scared. You need to know this information and be ready. You can still have what you want. It is important that you are simply aware that no

Don't Believe It!

matter what field you wish to pursue, power is a big game and you need to know the rules before you get in. But get in! What can you do against all this? Stay tuned for the second section of this book. But for the moment start by not believing the Power Peddlers when they tell you:

1. that they can control your destiny.
2. that you are a piece of meat.
3. that you are only worth the profit you make them.
4. that you can't work because they support someone else.
5. that you should have called your understudy.

Chapter 9

The Muck Merchants

An editor——a person employed on a newspaper, whose business it is to separate the wheat from the chaff, and see that the chaff is printed.
-Elbert Hubbard

The final source of negative information doesn't come from people you necessarily know or work with. Yet it can be more difficult to combat because it is so well organized. Great resources of time and money are spent to pump trash into your home and ultimately

Don't Believe It!

into your brains. It comes through pieces of paper delivered to your doorstep, or through a little box in your front room. Unbelievable amounts of money are spent per second to influence you through this medium. Interestingly, it is generally referred to as the media.

My first experience with the media was when I was eight years old. I had gotten stuck in an elevator and a lovely article appeared about my tragedy. Wow, I was famous! True accomplishment! Recognition! Unknown to me at eight was that the primary goals of the media are to suck you in, scramble your brains and spit you out.

Through the media, endless streams of negative drivel assault your senses and chew up your mind with what are ironically called "sound bites". These sound bites are short pieces of information that hold the maximum amount of garbage possible. It's too expensive to have any thoughtful discussions through the media, so it's crammed into meaninglessness which is often mistaken for intelligent communication by the public. Most of the public is unaware that this nonsense smothers their senses and subsequently brainwashes them, turning them into mind-numbed robots.

Whether we are talking about the news, or the endless parade of human degradation on talk shows, it is mostly the same. They generally promote the idea that we are all victims, unable to control our own lives. These shows worship disaster, heartbreak, perversion, hatred, disrespect, helplessness, and atrocity. Many of these blind guides actually think they are doing a public service. And yet their goals are simple: destroy faith in human accomplishment, demolish the hope that we can change and improve our lives, and crush love and human kindness. They say they are simply presenting the facts. But facts often vary depending on the perspective of the person interpreting them. Sure, people get killed. But I would say that more people participate in acts of love than acts of murder. Yet, for some reason love doesn't sell newspapers. Why? Is kindness not as exciting as homicide? What's worse is that the public starts believing that what they see through the media is the way the world is. It is not. It is trash, pure and simple. Am I being harsh and fanatical? You bet. Because I believe that this is the principal way the public soul is slowly being poisoned to death.

  The victim mentality is spreading through the world like a cancer. More and more people are being converted to the idea that their behavior cannot be controlled and their desires cannot be changed. They are most content when the media "experts" (on the payroll to sensationalize the worst) create labels for their particular helpless behavior. The label seems to protect these people with victim personalities from personal responsibility. It tells them that it's not their fault because they were "born that way." They continue in their meaningless quest to discover "who they are," never realizing that who they are is both malleable and impermanent. People can always change any aspect of their personalities, behaviors, and desires. You must not believe anyone who tells you can't.

  These labels are easy sound bites, and when inundated by them enough times, we may begin believing that every expert and fellow citizen has accepted them as well. When something happens often enough, and we don't know the cause, we want a label. When babies cry a lot, we call it colic. Yet no scientist

Don't Believe It!

has definitely determined what colic is. When people have a problem for which there is no clear scientific understanding of its cause, people start bandying around words like syndrome or disorder. They even start saying that those with the problem are "diagnosed" and that they should be accepted for who they are and what they have. People seem to want closure to their helplessness. They need a label that tells them that it's not their fault and that there is nothing they can do about it. Don't get me wrong! I do believe people have serious problems, but I seriously object to labels. When people are labeled rather than distinguished for their behavior, there is a tendency for the person to feel powerless. A label creates an air of intellectual approval for these feelings. People, almost with glee, can be heard bragging about their personal label of impotency. It would be better to focus on the answer to their problem than on an unscientific diagnosis.

It may be a bitter pill to swallow but most of the time the only thing that stands between you and change is your belief that you can change. This basic principal is imperative to understand in order to achieve your dreams. Here is the rule: All appetites, passions, moods, desires, and emotions can eventually be managed and changed. Some may take a while, but they can still be changed. It is dangerous to believe you are an exception to this rule, because, as I said before, some things are so difficult to change that the only thing motivating continued effort is faith, hope, and a belief that you can change. Don't forget that. Never give up on becoming the person you truly want to be just because some Muck Merchant on television has told you to accept yourself for "who you are." You can be who and what you wish to be.

The Muck Merchants

Also, be careful joining organizations that are filled with people with your present problem. Many of these organizations can offer various wonderful ways of overcoming your problem, make you feel like you're not alone, and offer you loving support. However, they can also backfire as you begin surrounding yourself with people with the same problem and start identifying with them. You start thinking of yourself as "one of them." As you continue this self-identification process, you start to think like them. The best way to change is to surround yourself with the people you want to become like and not the people you don't want to become like. If you want to become thin, surround yourself with naturally thin people. Get inside their brains, see what they do. If you want to be wealthy, start friendships with people who are wealthy and see how they think differently from the rest of the world. Stop focusing on the mistakes and get to the answers.

The media is committed to focusing on problems and not solutions. What would the world be like if the media were to spend even 50% of its time focusing on people that overcame great opposition in the face of disaster or affliction? Isn't this news too? Watch the evening news (only once) and count how many stories are about murders, robbery, natural disasters, wars, famine, infidelity, and hate. The list goes on. Yet, if they feel the need to discuss these things, how much harder would it be to find someone that went out of the way to lend a helping hand in the face of these tragedies? But it doesn't sell newspapers...or so they say.

If you allow yourself to be surrounded by these influences, you too will start to get a nasty little picture of this world that will begin to erode your ability to

Don't Believe It!

believe in your dreams. So turn off the cynical soap operas, the toxic talk shows, the negative news, and cancel your subscription to your nefarious newspaper. Instead, write your own news. Create your own reality. Don't believe the Muck Merchants when they tell you:

1. that you cannot change.
2. that the world is a nasty place.
3. that you are surrounded by evil people.
4. that you are encompassed by disasters.
5. that you need to be labeled.
6. that success only comes to a chosen few.
7. that success comes by picking that lucky lotto number.
8. that true accomplishment arrives when you get stuck in an elevator.

Section 2

The Risk Taker

*Our doubts are traitors,
And make us lose
the good we oft might win,
By fearing to attempt.
--Shakespeare*

Chapter 10

The Ask-For-What-You-Wanter

Ask, and it shall be given you....
-Matt. 7:7

Now the fun begins! After telling you about all of the negative people to avoid, it's time to tell you what to do to achieve your dreams. Unfortunately, after a lifetime of negative influences and programming, the biggest Dream Killer you face may be yourself. What you believe will either bring you closer to or further from the desires you seek. Therefore, some reprogramming may be in order. Almost all of us need this reprogramming. Most of us are plagued with beliefs that keep us from our dreams. Fortunately, these beliefs don't have to be with us forever. As we stop believing in these impotent ideas, we become Risk Takers. Bringing anything unique and exceptional to the world requires risk. It requires the use of your creative intellect. It rejects the tried and true and spurns the safe and secure ways of meandering through life. Frankly, it takes guts to put yourself up to open criticism by the public. It takes emotional risk to face rejection and failure. The truth is, you are either creating and expanding, or you are becoming part of the world's problems as you subject yourself to intellectual and emotional atrophy. As we challenge universal entropy through our creative powers, we assert our true natures. We are born creators. As we use these powers to assert our dreams and desires, we discover the basis of our ability to feel joy.

One of the first things my mother taught me was to always ask for what I wanted. She would teach me to go to the people who had the power to grant me my desires and just simply ask. If she sensed a little fear on my part, she would say, "Well, Dan, all they can say is 'no.'" If I didn't ask, the answer might as well have been "no."

My mother learned a lot of this philosophy from her father, who was an expert at selling and dealing. My grandfather used to take me to the huge local flea market that stretched for miles. We would spend the day there, and he would teach me how to bargain and get what I wanted for the price I wanted to pay. He taught me to keep a straight face and ask for what I wanted, without embarrassment or shifting my gaze.

The Ask-For-What-You-Wanter

He told me to determine ahead of time how much I was willing to pay, cut it in half and then cut it in half again. Then one day, he gave me some change and sent me out into the market alone to test his teachings. I was young so he would stay behind and watch me from a distance. On my first try, I found a big stuffed dog that I wanted. I walked up to the seller and noticed that it had a price tag of $11. Without being fazed, I looked the man in the eye and offered him a dollar fifty. He looked me over and said, "Don't you know this goes for eleven bucks?" I didn't blink or change my expression. "I have a dollar fifty for the dog." He seemed dumbfounded. His wife looked at him and said, "Aw, give the kid his dog." We made our exchange and continued through the market. In the end, I came home with a number of great toys I had purchased for a pocket full of coins. Everywhere I went, people seemed overpowered by some mysterious force that defied their reason. I began to see firsthand that asserted desire was power. Asking without fear somehow mollified people's hardened self-interest.

I continued to use this principle as I grew older. As I neared completion of my bachelor's degree, I had completed all but my senior recital. I had entered the opera major late and had only completed a couple of years of voice lessons. As a means of taking the pressure off of the senior recital, the faculty held a final jury three weeks before the concert to tell you whether or not you passed. After singing for the faculty, I waited for forty-five minutes as they deliberated. I was led back in. The judges were sitting behind a table, hands folded, stony faced. One of them spoke and told me that after careful deliberation, they had decided not to let me graduate. Regardless of whether it was in my

Don't Believe It!

best interest to let me go, they told me that it would be embarrassing for the university if I applied for a master's degree elsewhere and didn't seem prepared. Unabashed, I looked them all in the eye and said, "Look, I've finished all of my class work. There is nothing else to keep me here except your opinion about my singing today. I respectfully request that you make an exception to your rule and judge me from the actual concert in three weeks." I was matter-of-fact and didn't avert my gaze. They looked at one another and when they once again met my eyes, I knew that I had graduated. As far as being ready to apply to a graduate program at my next university, I was the only one out of all the others applying that passed all sections of the graduate entrance examination.

Soon after I had finished my graduate work, the General Director of a large opera company came to my town. He had been hearing auditions throughout the U. S. His company was on the other side of the country, and the operas were performed in a two thousand-seat house. The tenor who got the lead role would sing for some 14,000 people and receive some national recognition, be reviewed by *Opera News*, and receive other important exposure. I went into the audition a bit nervous. After my audition I was asked to return to audition again. Later, still unsure about my lack of professional experience, the director informed me that to be considered for this role further, I would have to fly down to southern California to sing for him a third time. I bought the plane ticket and spent a couple of hours singing for him. I had a cold at the time and after about an hour, my voice was fast disappearing. I didn't want to tell him that I was sick because that's considered bad business in the opera world. You either don't audition or you do. Companies don't like to hire sickly people. He assumed that it was just bad technique. He was more unsure than ever. We got into his car and he took me back to the airport. After having expressed his grave doubts about me he became silent. It seemed my efforts and money had been vain. But then, I realized that I hadn't asked for what I want. He pulled into the airport and stopped his car. I drew a big breath and said, looking him in the eye, "Look, give me this job. I know I can do it and I want you to know that I can do it. Hire me." As I stared at him, he averted his gaze. The next day, his assistant called me to negotiate the contract.

Big opportunities don't come along very often in people's lives. However, you should practice the technique of asking for what you want when small opportunities present themselves on a daily basis. Whether you are at the grocery store, hair salon, or the post office, there's always an opportunity to kindly yet directly assert your desires. When the big opportunities come, you'll be ready.

There is nothing worse than people who talk to others as if they were walking on glass. If you have to walk on eggshells when you talk to people, don't talk to them. They will not only notice your fear, but will be offended by it. You will telegraph to them that you expect them to respond badly. They will fulfill your expectations every time. When your eyes dart to and fro, and your words take the circuitous route, you insult the person with whom you are speaking. Don't look apologetic when you say anything to anyone. If you feel apologetic before you even open your mouth, don't open your mouth.

If you want to achieve your dreams, be direct. Ask for what you want, trusting that you will get what

Don't Believe It!

you request.
    Don't believe that:

1. you can't ask for exactly what you want.
2. you can't get what you want after they say "no."
3. you should be embarrassed to ask for your dreams.
4. rejection is a big deal.
5. people's opinions of you are more important than your opinion of yourself.
6. you can't get a big stuffed dog for a buck fifty.

Chapter 11

The Unapproachables Approacher

*Give me the young man who has brains
enough to make a fool of himself.*
    -Robert Louis Stevenson

There are some people in our society that seem so wealthy, powerful, or occupied that we are afraid to approach them. They may be movie stars, business executives, politicians, or idols of ours that just seem too far out of reach from us normal folk. You may see them on television or in the papers, which makes them

Don't Believe It!

somehow not seem to be real.

As I stated earlier, it's very important to get advice from people who either have achieved your goal or are living the life you would like to live. (Never take advice from others. It's just a bunch of useless opinions.) But how do you approach these people?

I remember when I first saw a famous person. I was fourteen and attending a summer camp at a university. I was busy eating lunch in a local dormitory cafeteria when in walked another teenager. This was no ordinary teenager but one I had seen a hundred times on television and in the movies. I was awestruck. As this teen idol sat down with his tray, I wondered what he was doing in this stupid little cafeteria. Suddenly girls from all over the room shot up out of their seats and ran over to him. they began asking for autographs and pictures. Actually, they didn't really ask. As flashbulbs went off around this young man, he tried to eat and ignore them. The cameras caught him in some of the most unflattering poses as food filled up his cheeks. He vainly tried not to answer questions with his mouth full. All of a sudden I felt sorry for him. The glamour fell away, and I saw a boy that ate food just like I did. Unfortunately, although he had the same physical needs as I, he didn't have the privacy. I realized that he was human and approachable. At this point, I began to question the validity of advertising. People were just people. The media had lied. Awe was created to sell tickets.

In spite of this discovery, I still believe in respect. I do believe that those who have achieved a great deal deserve respect and admiration. But we run into danger when we dehumanize them and make them gods. There is no one on earth whom we should fear approaching.

The Unapproachables Approacher

During my graduate work in San Jose, I heard word in the halls that Irene Dalis, General Director of Opera San José, was looking in New York for a tenor to sing the lead in the next opera. She was a retired opera singer, once the highest paid mezzo-soprano in the world. I had seen her at the university and local events several times during my two years there. Whenever she walked into a room, everyone knew it. She carried herself with an energy and power that scared me to death. She had heard me sing over those two years, but had barely said "hello" to me. She was an organized woman and when she wanted to convey a message to someone, she would generally do it through a subordinate. If anyone seemed unapproachable to me, it was she. She ran a tight ship, one of the few opera companies in the U.S. to stay always in the black.

The students at the university were generally scared of her as well. But when I heard of the tenor search through the rumor mill, I knew what I had to do. I had never sung an opera in a foreign language before, but how does anybody get their first break?

She had an office at the university and I found a time when she was there. I went to the door and knocked. She opened it, her electricity came flooding out and almost knocked me down. I asked if I could have a moment. "Okay, what can I do for you," she said firmly as she walked away, lit up a cigarette, and sat down behind her desk. I said, "I am aware that you have been searching around the U.S. for a tenor in the next opera." She blew out a stream of smoke and forcefully prodded, "And..." "And," I said, "I don't want you to look any more. I can do the part and I want you to know that I can do it. Give me the job." She pulled

Don't Believe It!

the cigarette out of her mouth, looked me up and down, raised a single eyebrow and said, "Oh yes?" I returned the ball, "Yes." A smile crept across her face as she inflected her voice, "Really? Okay, I'm the boss. You've got the job. I'll tell the conductor and stage director you've got the job." Just like that. She later became one of the biggest supporters of my career.

But what if she had said no? I wouldn't have the job anyway. What if I hadn't asked? But I did! The results of that one moment still echo through my life.

One of the most difficult things about approaching those who can really help you, is that they can be hard to reach. Asking for what you want is often the easy part. Getting past the middleman, the secretary or the agent can be the hard part. Often there are tiers of middlemen. Each one evaluates your work and decides whether your request or idea should be passed on to the next level. Sadly, if you sell your idea to the first level, you can bet they will not turn around and sell it to the next. Instead, they will present your idea in the most disinterested way possible. This is so they can protect themselves. If their superiors reject the idea, they don't lose face. In other words, it is a complete waste of time to trust your dreams to an intermediary. They will not sell you. You must sell yourself and your dreams directly to those who can make the final decision.

One of my dreams had been to sing at San Francisco Opera on the stage of the War Memorial Opera House. When I was in high school, our orchestra would take a yearly trip to see the symphony perform there. I was awe-struck by the building and the beauty of the entire experience.

When I finally got an agent, I asked him for months to call San Francisco Opera to see if I could make a debut. The company had already heard me sing, but I needed some follow-up and salesmanship. After many months, I realized my agent was afraid to sell me to such a prestigious opera house. After all, some of the biggest names in the business sang there. Who was I? My agent had a reputation to protect as well. So I saved him the humiliation and called the Artistic Administrator myself. Once on the phone, I mentioned my dream and my availability. Remembering me, she said, "Oh, are you available? We were looking for your voice type for an upcoming opera." Bingo. Walking on that stage filled one of my lifelong dreams. Of course, my agent took a percentage.

The moral is: Always learn to approach the unapproachables and stop believing that:

1. you need to share your dreams with a middleman.
2. you need to talk to a middleman at all.
3. you can't talk to important people.
4. you shouldn't go straight to the top with your requests.
5. you're less of a human being than another human being.
6. just because you talk with your mouth full, you can't become a famous movie star.

Chapter 12

The Approval Infringer

*We can easily forgive a child who is
afraid of the dark; the real tragedy of life
is when men are afraid of the light.*
— *Plato*

Okay, so you've got guts. You can ask people for what you want and you don't have a problem with approaching the bigwigs of the world. You feel comfortable with all kinds of people. The question now arises, how do you feel about doing things that make others feel uncomfortable? Every culture has certain social mores. There are unwritten laws by which we live when we are among friends, family, colleagues, mentors, and employers. There are things that some

Don't Believe It!

people won't do because no one else does them. There are other things that people won't do because of tradition, fear, or a simple lack of invitation.

While some people are waiting for invitations and approvals, the Risk Takers are creating their own invitations and giving themselves approval. They're breaking the rules, taking the initiative, and often risking embarrassment. They don't always ask for permission. They admit mistakes quickly and get on with their lives. They make quick decisions without giving themselves a chance to fear. When the options seem to run out, they do the unexpected or the unorthodox.

None of this means that Risk Takers break the law or feel a worthy end justifies any means. Rather, it means that they will often break unwritten rules of convention and fear that keep society from productivity. This can be difficult to do at first.

One of my first opportunities to risk came when I decided to play the piano in the high school "gong show." An imitation of the television show, it featured three judges and a very large gong. The judges would rate you from one to ten unless you were awful. That's where the gong came in. I was playing in front of about two thousand gong-hungry high school students and had gotten about halfway through the song. Suddenly, one of the judges (also a high school student) stood up with the mallet gesturing to the audience. Many were yelling, "Gong him!" I saw that crowd mentality was growing against the possibility of me finishing my song. The judge was poised for the swing. My heart was beating fast. What could I do?

Suddenly, I jumped to the last three measures of the song and abruptly finished. Everyone seemed a bit stunned, but I had forced them to score me. As a result, I won my first competition. It was a small unorthodox move that had paid off. It wasn't that bad. I decided to take more risks.

After high school, I got a summer job working at an amusement park. After working on "The Lobster" half the summer, I was transferred to the Grand Music Hall to act as an usher. When I saw the show, I was envious. I could do what they were doing on stage. Kids my age were singing and dancing, and I wanted to do that. My feelings were shared by an usherette. We began to get tired of telling people where the bathroom was or whether or not they can bring food into the theater. We had seen the show a hundred times and had it completely memorized. I spoke to the director and mentioned that I knew the show and if any one got sick.... Well, you know. No one did. So one day when my friend and I were assigned outside to crowd control, we decided to do something that might fulfill our desire to be on stage. It would probably have been against the rules, had we asked. We didn't of course. We performed the show for the waiting crowd outside. People threw money. My first professional performing job! It was also a great lesson in the joys of capitalism.

By the time I got to college, I needed another job. I wanted something that could use my music skills and allow me to be on campus. I went to the university employment office at the beginning of the semester. Big mistake. Here's how it worked:

1. You went to one room and looked at posted jobs.
2. You filled out a registration form in another room.
3. You went to the end of a line with 200 people in it.
4. When you got to the front, you handed in your registration form.

Don't Believe It!

5. You got in another line to speak to a counselor.
6. Once with the counselor, you were interviewed.
7. If found worthy for the job, the counselor called the department offering the job.
8. You crossed the campus to the appropriate department and handed your recommendation card to a secretary.
9. The secretary looked at the appointment book and you set an appointment to be interviewed.
10. You came back and had your interview for the job if someone else hadn't gotten the job by this time.
11. If you got the job, the person interviewing you signed a card you had to bring back to the employment office. (Where you would wait in line again.)

These were the "rules." This was the procedure. What did I do? I checked the job board, found the job playing the piano for ballet classes, guessed where it was on campus, went to the head of the department, avoiding the secretary, and got the job. The person who hired me then completed the paperwork for me and sent it to the employment office. She was happy because they had classes going without a pianist and needed me right away. In essence, she had been waiting in line as well.

Employers and administrators constantly make rules. But there are always times when rules get in the way of the efficiency they were intended to promote. It has always made me laugh when an employer or administrator who has created a rule has told me, "Those are the rules." I always have retorted with the question, "Didn't you make the rule?" or "Who made the rule?" followed by the quick rejoinder, "Don't you have the power to make exceptions to the rules?"

The Approval Infringer

When someone resorts to a "those are the rules" kind of answer, he has abandoned the reason the rule was implemented in the first place. Thus, we have the constant debates over the spirit verses the letter of the law. It's usually just a power thing. The minute people get a little authority or power, they hold on to it for dear life until you give them another opportunity to exert it in a different direction.

University life gave me a lot of wonderful opportunities to break convention and take risks. By the time I was finished, my risking skills had become more finely tuned. This is not to say that I always succeeded when I risked. But rather, I wasn't afraid to fail. Failure had become an opportunity to learn and grow.

After a while, I was on my own. I wanted to continue singing, and I wanted an agent. I was in California and knew very little about the business end of my career. (Another thing college doesn't teach you.) Many of my colleagues had auditioned for agents, but hadn't gotten any bites. I was surrounded by negativity about the competition for agents and jobs in the U.S. I was told there were too many singers and not enough opportunities.

Exasperated with this drivel, I got on a plane for New York. I gave myself ten days with no previous appointments, preparation or leads. As soon as I checked into my hotel, I got on the phone and started dialing. I found some accompanists and picked their brains. I asked them where they were accompanying and which opera companies were in town. One of the largest opera companies in the U.S. was in town, and I found out where agents would be presenting their wares. I called the company, out of state, and asked if

Don't Believe It!

anyone had canceled. Indeed they had, at 4:20 P.M. I showed up, grabbed a pianist from the hall, and crashed the audition. When I walked in, I confidently said, "I am the replacement for your 4:20 cancellation." I handed him my resume and sang. After the song, I was asked if I would like to be the leading man opposite Cecilia Bartoli, one of the world's leading coloratura mezzos. Just like that. Within a few more days, I had a contract to make my Lincoln Center debut and three immediate offers from agents. I had done about fifteen auditions in ten days. Ms. Bartoli soon flew out to San Francisco and we sang through some of the opera together--my first experience singing next to a star. It was a great thrill. Of course, I might never have gotten on the plane for New York in the first place. What a crazy risk! You bet. That's how it works.

It's time for you to stop believing that:

1. you need to ask permission for everything you do.
2. your action requires the approval of others.
3. you can't take risks that your colleagues or friends wouldn't take.
4. you can't take risks that your mentors or idols wouldn't take.
5. you can avoid disapproval when you start to do important things.
6. you have to wait for an invitation.
7. someone has to call you first. Call them!
8. you have to stand in lines.
9. you have to fill out application forms before you get a job.
10. you have to go through a chain of command.
11. you can't start dancing and singing in the middle of an amusement park.

Chapter 13

The Hoop Hater

*Time is a great teacher,
but unfortunately it kills all its pupils.
-Hector Berlioz*

When I was a dog, I jumped through hoops. No, this isn't about reincarnation or hypnotic regression. It was one of my first opera jobs. I would clothe myself in fur and doggy makeup, go to schools and sing:

I'm a dog, ruff-ruff
I'm a dog, ruff-ruff

Don't Believe It!

I'm eager, faithful, and true.
Trotting by my master's side
'Cause that's what I'm supposed to do.

You might say that I was "paying my dues." If I barked well, next time I might get to bark in Italian.

I hate jumping through hoops. It's generally a waste of time. However, something can be said for proving your loyalty and lending a helping hand. Singing in doggese made the kids happy and helped out the local opera company's outreach program. However, I can't say that it prepared me for the stage. Maybe a bit. Some hoops are okay to jump through.

Some are not. As you begin to follow your personal path, you will cross the paths of others on their own paths. Some of them can help you, but a lot of them will use you to further their own agendas. If you are particularly weak-minded, you can actually end up spending a good portion of your life pursuing the goals of others. There is no better example of this than the field of education. I know that I keep harping on the educational system, but it's important that you know how it works.

When you go to school, you learn something called a curriculum. That's a fancy word for "You will study what I think is important for you." A curriculum is set up by educators who have their own paths, own agendas and own priorities. They often believe that a student's life must reflect their own values in terms of goals and intellectual interests. So they set up these required classes, whether or not they meet an individual student's needs. I have no objection to suggested courses for study, provided a student can question and request to change the course for legitimate reasons. Generally, however, the student's needs and desires are the last priority in the world of education.

It all begins very young. For a time, I taught a full kindergarten curriculum as I was working on my Master's degree. I was excited because the job was in a private school that boasted an advanced program of learning. Most of the children were a few grades ahead of their public school counterparts in SAT testing. I worked in a co-teacher environment and had about twenty-five students. As the year progressed, I noticed that a number of the students were bored with the curriculum. They were getting perfect scores on all of the tests and would finish early. One little boy in particular was getting to be a discipline problem. The other teacher immediately said, "Let's do our best to get rid of him. Let's get him kicked out of the school." However, when I looked at him, I saw myself, bored to tears. I went home and developed a new math program for about six of the most bored students. They had actually finished the year's math program, and the year was barely half over. So I taught these five-year-olds algebra. I created work sheets and tests with up to ten-level problems that included multiplication and division of variables. They ate it up. They all got perfect scores on all these tests as well. The young boy stopped being a problem. All this caught the attention of the upper-level math professor, who was not only amazed when he saw the tests, but started advertising this around the school and administrators. My co-teacher got angry. She came up to me and accused me of taking credit for the success of these students, when she was also their teacher. The next thing I knew, I was in with the principal and the superintendent as my co-teacher began fabricating stories about my work with the

Don't Believe It!

students. She complained about the little boy I had worked with and succeeded in getting him to leave the school. Then I was ordered to cease and desist my work on math. I was told that, according to every scholarly work, what I was doing was impossible for a five-year-old to comprehend. Then they said that I was no longer allowed to work with these six children until every one in the class was up to their level. Although I spent equal time with all the students, it was for some reason anathema to these administrators to imagine any inequality of results. They insisted that all students must be on the same level. Unfortunately, equality of opportunity doesn't always yield equality of result. Yet the agenda of the school, although progressive, was to hold students back from their potential to create artificial equality.

Schools will often allow personal potential to suffer in favor of their curriculum. This continues throughout the university. However, there are ways around it. Most universities will allow you to test out of classes or even to waive them if you learn how and whom to ask. When I was doing my undergraduate work, I did this often if I felt I didn't need the class, or it didn't bring me closer to my career goals. This ruffled some feathers along the way. One teacher was so upset when I tried to test out of his class that he informed me, after I had completed three-quarters of the exam, that I would receive a poor grade no matter how well I fared on the exam. He also told me that he knew I tried to "get out of things" and that the only reason I hadn't been kicked out of the university was because I was so talented. That was the point, wasn't it? If I wasn't different, I might have needed his class. I made the mistake of getting angry and telling him that I thought his class was a waste of time. He threw me out of his office and screamed, "Dan Montez, as long as I teach at this university, you will never pass my class and never graduate." I did graduate and never had to take his "required class." I found a way to get the class waived.

I should never have lost my temper. However, teachers need to see that each student is different. We each have specific goals and the university should serve those goals. However, you notice that I have not complained about my general education courses. I enjoyed them all very much and have used the general knowledge much in my life. My "beef" is with specific departmental curricula.

During my graduate work, I discovered that the curriculum was largely dictated by the classes the faculty wanted to teach. The professors that made decisions on curriculum were the same teachers that taught the classes none of the students were interested in. I had received a report on the desires of the students regarding their curriculum and found that only one student of all graduate students wanted and felt they needed the classes being taught by those making the curriculum decisions. In other words, if they voted to create a curriculum to support the goals and desires of the students, they would be voting themselves right out of a job. Once I figured this out, I went to one of these decision-making professors and discussed it with him. Still unable to always keep my mouth shut, I ended the conversation with, "So, therefore you would be voting yourself out of a job, is that right?" Caught red-handed, he became red-faced. I had blown it again. Luckily, he didn't try to keep me from graduating, but I did end up jumping through a hoop. In order to learn what I wanted to learn, my graduate work stretched to approximately sixty units,

Don't Believe It!

twice the number required to finish a Master's degree. Why did I waste my time? I'm not sure. No one has ever asked me about my education during an audition. In fact, opera companies generally insist that you leave it off of your program biography. It has nothing to do with what you produce.

Stop jumping through hoops! Learn to learn what you want. Love to learn and educate yourself about the world around you. Don't depend on others to teach you. Teach yourself. Teachers are tools. Education is a tool. The more you know, the more power you will have. But don't be dictated to. You know what you need to know better than anyone else. It's important to keep an open mind and listen to suggestions, but equally important to set boundaries. You could spend your entire life in a library studying a trillion different subjects from around the globe and yet do nothing. If you don't use your knowledge to add something to the world or to make it better, it is all self-indulgent nonsense. Learn to spend time learning, then learn to spend time using and doing. Avoid the detours set up by the agendas of others. Your life is too short to spend much of it climbing someone else's mountain.

Don't believe that:

1. you have to do things that are of no value to you or your future.
2. you have to support someone else's agenda.
3. you have to learn what others believe is important for you to learn.
4. you can't skip steps.
5. you have to sing the "dog aria" to get to the top.

Chapter 14

The Fall-on-your-Facer

*Truth emerges more readily
from error than from confusion.'
—Francis Bacon*

If by now you've gotten the impression that I never make big mistakes or never make a fool of myself, it's only because I would love you to have that impression. Now I'll come clean. The truth is I could write ten more books on all of my failures and embarrassments. But that's how I have learned.

Don't Believe It!

You don't succeed unless you learn, you don't learn unless you risk, and you don't risk without falling on your face again and again.

A new fine arts facility was opening in my hometown and, at age eighteen, I was asked to play at the formal grand opening on their newly acquired grand piano. I had recently memorized the first movement of Beethoven's Pathetique Sonata, a well known standard in recital repertory. I was to play it in my first important public appearance. My teacher, an icon of the community, was in the audience in her best dress. The lights dimmed and I walked out. I played through the whole piece flawlessly--until I reached the last five chords. Suddenly I looked at my hands and my mind went blank. I had no clue how to end the piece and hundreds of people were staring at me who knew this famous piece. I improvised. I made up the ending and ended in C Major instead of C Minor with a big ragtime finish. The tragic piece suddenly had a snappy ending. After the hesitant applause of the audience, my teacher could only say, "Well, that was interesting."

How could I ever play again? People had paid money to hear me. I couldn't be trusted, let alone trust myself again. I once asked my teacher why she didn't perform. She told me that it was because she got too nervous. I understood that. Sharing who you are with the world was mostly psychological. I had previously thought it was just practice.

What is this thing called nerves? Why do people get stage fright? Why do we care what other people think? I have come to believe that all people must face these questions before they truly succeed. Most people would rather hide in a closet or cubicle and privately do their work in safety from public scrutiny. Working for yourself means taking responsibility for your own work.

The Fall-on-your-Facer

This, for many, is the most frightening thing of all. But I believe we were born to risk, born to fall on our faces, and born to get up again after we fall, standing even taller.

After my first semester of voice lessons, I was required to sing in front of a "jury." Does that sound like a nice relaxing experience? Professors sit behind a table with pencils in hand, and they analyze you while you sing. The first time I did this, I opened my mouth to sing and choked. My first piano jury was the same. My legs shook so badly that I couldn't keep my foot on the pedal and my hands were so distressed that they decided to hit everything but the notes in the music.

Fear was my major problem. I could perform so much better in a private practice room. Almost everyone is that way when they begin. We do so much better by ourselves than in front of others. We love to sing in the shower. There are so many talented people in the world that do not share what they have with the world because of fear. I believe that those that hide their talents because of the fear of others are extremely selfish and egotistical. We were born to face our egos and our fears, understand them, and overcome the bondage in which they hold us.

Personally, I got angry. I decided to figure out what I was afraid of and how to overcome it. So, I began reading books on fear, stage fright, and self-image. I bought tapes on self-hypnosis and relaxation. I went to a bio-feedback lab. There, they would hook electrodes up to me and monitor my body temperature and heart rate. I would practice willing my heart rate and temperature to change. I talked to other performers. Most of all, I refused to run away. I decided that I would embrace the idea of falling on my

Don't Believe It!

face. I would learn to love making a fool of myself in front of others. I should keep going on stage despite how I felt. Risk would be the rule.

After I graduated and auditioned for my first opera in a new city, I could sing but I couldn't act. But the fall-on-my-face rule was still in place. I didn't expect, however, that it would almost literally be realized. At my first audition, the stage director said, "So you can sing. Let's see how you use the stage. Sing it again, but this time, use this chair." He put a chair in the middle of the room and asked the pianist to begin. I had never had an acting class and had no idea what to do. For some insane reason, I lifted my leg to step over the chair and... tumbled over it. I believe when I left the room I could hear them laughing. In fact, I had provided such entertainment that they gave me the job. Personally, I like to think that they could see that I must have been a Risk Taker to make such an enormous fool of myself. Even when you fail, you succeed!

Most every famous person in the world has lists of rejection stories. I love reading about them-- everything from Colonel Sanders having 1009 restaurants reject his chicken recipe to the thousands of failed light bulbs built by Edison. The big difference between these people and those that don't succeed is that they just try again. They never give up. They try a new way. They get up again after they fall.

Anytime you try something new, you take the risk of falling on your face. So get used to it and it won't seem so bad. After you begin risking, try to maintain a habit. It's a good idea to always be trying new things, working on new goals, and learning new skills. It's also a better idea to find things that test your fears. Especially those that draw public attention and criticism. The willingness to fail and expose your inner self in front of others will teach you more than any book you read in your closet.

There's much to learn about how to do all of this fearlessly, but for the moment, learn to do it with fear. As you learn the private reasons you fear and then face those fears, they will slowly dissipate into the nothingness that they are. Learn to reject the belief that:

1. you can be successful without falling on your face.
2. you will succeed more than you fail.
3. any failure is final.
4. you can't get up again when you fall.
5. failing in front of a large group needs to devastate you.
6. everyone will like your offering to the world.
7. falling on your face can't be fun.
8. that you will always get a job after you trip over a chair.

Chapter 15

The Goal Setter

*He flung himself upon his horse
and rode madly off in all directions.
-Stephen Leacock*

When I was a teenager, my parents and I visited a local county fair one afternoon. Only a few people were there at this time of day. Seeing there were no lines, I decided to try one of the rides. I went up to the man taking the tickets and noticed that no one else was on the ride. The ride looked like a tipped ferris wheel

Don't Believe It!

with dangling cars that resembled little mushrooms. I got into one of the metallic toadstools. As the ride started to move, my car began to swoop high into the air as it picked up speed. Then it dove down quickly to the ground, leaving my stomach above me in the air. Unbeknownst to me, the man had decided to be kind and let me stay on the contraption for longer than the normal three minutes. He began using me as an advertisement. Nobody came. Around and around I went. I knew something was wrong. I began getting very ill. After about ten minutes, it became very painful. As I would pass the man on the downward dive, I would scream over and over, "Let me off! let me off! Let me oooooofff!"

Some people live lives like this. They travel in circles and confuse activity with accomplishment. Some are screaming, "Let me off! Let me off!" They're getting sick to their stomachs and realize that there must be more to life than this. They easily get stuck into ruts of activities that take them nowhere. Too many are just out to survive and get by. They may be very busy, but they lack one thing--focus.

During college, I must have changed my major focus about six times. I loved everything. For a time I was a computer science major; then it was languages, then religion. I had piano and voice scholarships simultaneously and had just applied for a composition scholarship. The next thing I knew, I was called in to speak to the head of the Music Department. He said, "You know, Dan, you're playing different areas in the department against one another. But beyond that, if you keep doing what you are doing, you'll be good at a lot of things, but you'll never be great at anything." Those words struck me hard. I knew I needed to choose.

The Goal Setter

At my piano lesson the following week, after playing a piece I had recently worked on, my piano professor sat back in his chair and said with an air of surprise, "Gee, you're good." I walked out of his office thinking to myself, "Wow. I've arrived. I don't need to do that anymore." That would free about four hours of practice per day from my schedule.

I always worked the hardest on things that people said I couldn't do. It may not be the best motivation one can have, but I loved to prove them wrong. I knew I was destined to choose the thing I was worst at! I loved the process. Arriving at the goal somehow always took the fight out of me.

Too many people in this world are more focused on the product than the process. Success requires a love for the details and an enjoyment of organizing them and putting them together.

These are the nuts and bolts of goal setting. How you set personal goals is the next big secret of success. There are so many wonderful books out there on how to do it and I recommend that you read as many as you can. There are as many different ways to set goals as there are people. However, there are some basic rules that most books agree upon:

1. you need them.
2. you need to write them down.
3. you need to begin with your long-term goals and end with the short-term goals.
4. set dates for completion.

Some actually think that they can meander around and end up on top of Mount Everest. But instead, you must have a specific idea of what you

Don't Believe It!

want. Don't hope that you can just work hard and then someday someone from the sweepstakes will knock on your door with a ten million dollar check.

Secondly, if you don't write them down, they're not real. That's why people are afraid to write them. If they fail, their failure becomes real as well. If they don't write them and they fail, they can just mumble that they weren't really their goals anyway. Write them. Read them regularly. I affirm to you that I would not have accomplished a tenth of the things I have had I not written my plans on paper.

Thirdly, the plan needs to begin with the end in mind. So many people do it backwards. They set admirable daily and weekly goals and hope they will lead them somewhere. They're not sure where, but the short-term goals sound so good that they are confident that something wonderful will come their way. Wrong! First, you need to write down your final destination. Then ask yourself where you will be right before that. There may be a lot of possibilities. Write them down. Continue with this process until you arrive at where you are now. You should end up with a number of paths that could lead you to your goal. You need to see the end from the beginning.

Will things get in the way if you map out such a detailed plan? Certainly. Things will change. You will have to make adjustments along the way. These are only minor course corrections. That's okay. Detours are fine as long as you start with a flight plan.

Finally, set dates. Even if you find that you needed longer to achieve your goal, it's still important to have them. If you had set the longer goal to begin with, you would have exerted less effort than with the shorter period of time. Therefore you still wouldn't make your goal in time. Setting time goals forces you to work harder than you would without them. Setting goals involves changing who you are. It involves continual learning and adaptation. All of these things take a strong will to develop habits.

When I teach voice students for the first time, the first thing I tell them is, "If you want to be a great singer, you have to have one strong ability—the ability to develop habits." Singing, like all other complex skills, involves hundreds of habits. A habit is something you do repeatedly without thinking about it. Your brain can handle only a few conscious activities at a time without going on overload. Kids know this when they try to pat their stomach and rub their heads at the same time. But if there are a hundred new skills that you have to do simultaneously in order to do something well, then they must become habits a few at a time. I always tell my students, "You may even get to the point where you can do what you want when you think about it, but can you do it when you don't think about it?" Making desirable traits automatic is the secret to changing who you are, and eventually, what you achieve.

Goals help you develop those habits one by one. You can't change overnight. Everything that has true value takes time. My first voice teacher always said to me, "Learn this: There's no such thing as insta-voice."

There are no magic pills, lucky numbers, or fortune cookies that will bring you success. There are no external sources you can count on. You can only count on your ability and desire to change yourself by forming new habits of thinking and acting.

Don't believe that:

1. you can succeed without goals.

Don't Believe It!

2. activity means accomplishment.
3. you don't need to develop new habits to reach your dream.
4. you don't need to focus.
5. you will get anywhere without a written road map.
6. you can go to a county fair without getting sick.

Chapter 16

The Attitude Enhancer

The greatest discovery of any generation is that a human being can alter his life by altering his attitude."
    -William James

My high school art instructor used to always tell the class, "If you're looking for sympathy, look under 'S.'" I always remembered that, perhaps because at the time it seemed like such a heartless thing to say. Or perhaps because I was always looking for sympathy. I grew up with somewhat of a victim personality. I complained a lot about how unfair life was. I remember getting angry when one of my teachers told me that life just wasn't fair. Acting like a victim worked for me. It got me a great deal of attention. I loved to get sick because of the kindness and sympathy it brought me.

It seemed that I was surrounded by ill health in my family. Many of my relatives always seemed to have diseases, allergies, and weight problems. In fact, one of my relatives was a fat lady in the circus.

When I was growing up, I assumed I was destined to join them. I was always sick and I always did everything I could to avoid physical education. I caught mononucleosis that kept me out of school for a while. Then I got hypoglycemia. I sprained an ankle just in time to get out of an unwanted P.E. class. By the time I was in college, I had gained about fifty pounds as I spent the evenings polishing off whole bags of potato chips and cream filled sandwich cookies.

When I left home I was on my own. It was at that point that I began a journey of change. I started to see the world in a different light and began to feel deeper yearnings for spirituality. My parents were great at teaching me many of the spiritual laws of happiness, but I only kept many of these laws superficially. I hadn't learned them from the inside out but rather from the outside in. I needed to be spiritual and not just look spiritual. I need to be positive and not just act positive.

As I took this personal journey, I confronted some of my most painful core beliefs. My health began to change. It began with the hypoglycemia. I previously needed to eat every two hours or I would black out. I finally had enough of this. After some deep spiritual struggles, I began to fast. Ultimately, I was able to go without food or water for forty continuous hours and still feel great. I began to reach my inner self.

As the years progressed, I rarely got sick. The fifty pounds came off as I began to study the minds and habits of naturally thin people. I stopped eating for psychological reasons. I began to exercise and enjoy it for the first time in my life. I started lifting weights. The first month of this was awful, but then I started to feel incredible. I couldn't get enough. It became almost a sacrament to me. The physical opposition necessary to create strength began to symbolize the spiritual and emotional opposition I faced which made me a stronger person.

About halfway to a black belt in Tae kwon do, my wife started getting a bit nervous during my tests. I was getting beaten up quite badly. Interestingly enough, I loved it! When I began training for a marathon, people would approach me and say, "Don't you know that people die and get heart attacks running a marathon? Don't you think you can exercise too much?" I would simply retort with, "A lot more people die every year sitting on the couch watching a soap opera while polishing off a bag of potato chips." Anyway, when I die, I hope it will be running a marathon or something similar. I hope I will be in the middle of pursuing a goal or attempting to accomplish something significant when I pass on. So many people are just sitting in their rocking chairs waiting for the big event.

As soon as you begin changing your life and your beliefs, many of the people who know you will question your goals. They like you the way you are. You are a predictable part of their life. Besides, they don't want to be "guilted" into changing their lives through your example.

As my life began to radically change because of the habits I had developed, people who didn't know me got nervous as well. I would practice the piano four hours a day, the voice another two, and had a full schedule at the university as well as outside jobs. Yet people would say, "Oh you're so talented! I could never do that. You must have been born with a gift." Believing that all talents are inborn makes so many people feel better about not trying. Heaven forbid if someone can develop a talent or a new set of habits. Sometimes I respond to these people, "How long would it take you to be as good as I am?" "Oh at least twenty years," they often say. Then I respond, "In twenty years, you'll either arrive there with the talent or without it. But you will arrive there one way or another."

Actually, making all of these changes is very hard. Motivation is everything. However, I am not "self-motivated" nor have I met anyone that is, frankly. Motivation is something we have to build like any other ability. We have to feed motivating things into our brains on a constant basis.

Have you ever gone to hear an inspiring speaker and walk out ready to take on the world? Then a few days later are you back in the same old rut feeling the way you used to? Learn this truth: Motivation doesn't last. That's why so many religions have weekly meetings. Inspiration is fleeting. We forget these feelings even from day to day.

So what do we do? First, we should act immediately when we are in the mood to act. Don't wait. The motivation to change yourself will be gone tomorrow. Secondly, we need to read books, listen to tapes, watch videos, go to PMA (Positive Mental

Attitude) seminars, see inspiring movies, listen to uplifting music, and make friends with positive people. You are surrounded by negativity everyday and you must counteract every piece of this garbage if you are to succeed.

Our environment eventually programs our brains. What we consider and believe affects our subconscious. Everyday we are making subconscious tapes that will be playing in the back of our heads for the rest of our lives. It's so much easier to program a brain than to reprogram a brain. Keep the bad stuff out. Put the good stuff in.

After I began writing and publishing positive material, I started getting phone calls of all kinds from around the U.S. One of the first that I received was from a man in California who called me in New York and began telling me his life story. He had read an article I had written on choosing how to feel and managing your emotions. He felt out of control and couldn't see how he could relax or be happy. He had just received a pay cut and didn't know how he would survive. I asked him how much he would now be making. To my surprise, it was about four times what I make every year. I had to keep myself from laughing from the irony. Here I was, giving him advice on being happy. It was a real eye opener to see that people can be happy or unhappy in just about any set of circumstances. Perspective is the key. What we believe brings us happiness and success faster than all of our hard work.

We need to get rid of our belief that:

1. motivation lasts.
2. you don't constantly need to fill your mind with

Don't Believe It!

positive, uplifting material.
3. there are really self-motivated people.
4. your attitude needs to be based on external events.
5. attitude is a minor player in the game of success.
6. I got mononucleosis from kissing.

Chapter 17

The Solution Seeker

The secret of success in life is for a man to be ready for his opportunity when it comes.
— *Benjamin Disraeli*

Once your attitude is under control, you'll begin to focus on all of the possibilities in your life and not on impossibilities. You will start to concentrate on solutions and stop dwelling on the problems. When you do this, the answers will come because you will get

Don't Believe It!

whatever you regularly focus our mind and attention on.

From a young age, I wanted to play the piano. But there were problems. My parents moved frequently and had financial difficulties. After about a year-and-a-half of lessons, I was on my own. I learned by myself how to play. When I was old enough to get a job, I started paying for my own lessons. My focus was on what I wanted and the solutions came. When someone wants something bad enough, they find a way.

By the time I wanted to go to college, my family couldn't send me. They couldn't even lend me any money. But I found someone who would. When times got tough at school and I had no money for books or food, my mother would make lollipops. My sisters would sell them everyday at school for a quarter and send me the money in the mail. Now, that's love. Love is a great motivator for solutions. Just when I would need help, it would always come. Instead of dwelling on our helplessness, we would always focus on a way to make it work.

Receiving help from others is one of the most common solutions we overlook. It's such a great thing to give, but I think receiving can be underrated. It can be such a humbling and loving experience. So many of us turn down help when it is offered because we have some sense of pride. Imagine me turning down my sisters after they had worked so hard to surprise me. I would have robbed them of an important joy as well. Anytime we don't accept a gift, we deprive the giver of an important experience. Our pride is foolish, because love needs to travel in both directions. It must be given and received. All of the success you achieve is not truly achieved on your own. You are helped by many others along the way. If you become wealthy, that money comes from people who believe in you or in what you have created. If you gain wisdom, you generally pick it up from many others. Many of us keep ourselves from success because we want to own it completely. We want to say we did it all by ourselves. We refuse help or even the opportunity itself that will bring us our dream. But it's impossible. We can't do it alone. Our egos will keep us in misery.

When I first came to New York to sing, I got out of rehearsal at Lincoln Center one evening and took the subway to Grand Central Station. It was about midnight and because of an emergency, they had closed down the tracks. I needed to get a train home. It was announced that one would be leaving instead from 125th Street. I didn't know the city at all and got on the wrong subway. As it went north, the people on the train started to make me nervous. As I approached my stop, a young man approached me and asked me if I actually intended on getting off at the next stop. I told him that I did and that I was going to catch a train at 125th Street. He told me that I was about four blocks off and had caught the wrong subway. We got off. Then he told me that we were in about the worst place we could be in New York City this time of night. He then informed me that he was from the neighborhood and that I better pretend that I know him and he would walk me to the train station. As we ascended above ground, I began noticing that there were gangs on every street corner, as well as drug dealers, prostitutes—you name it. We walked quickly and people began to stare at me because I obviously didn't fit in. I held my breath all the way to the train station. When we arrived, I thanked him, and he handed me a card which invited me to his church on Sunday. I don't question his

Don't Believe It!

intentions, nor do I care what they were. He had performed an act of kindness toward me and I was glad to accept the help.

As we trek toward our destinations, there are people out there who will help you through the scariest times. During many of the most difficult steps, we are carried along the way. There's nothing embarrassing about that. Many times we need to be carried, and that's when miracles happen. But many times they won't happen if we are not prepared to receive them. Preparation is a key to recognizing and receiving opportunities. Preparation is another key to creating solutions. People who focus instead on the problems generally just sit around waiting for opportunities they are not prepared to receive.

A couple of years after I got married, a friend of ours put us in touch with a business associate who was looking for someone to write the background music for a documentary. I hadn't really experienced the professional world but I thought the recommendation would be enough. I flew down to Hollywood and met with this man to discuss my ideas. He was very patient with me. He asked what I had done. "Nothing," I answered. He asked if I had any examples of my work. "No, but I'm good." He took me over to his stereo system and popped in a tape. Out came the most astounding fully orchestrated examples from all kinds of films. He told me that this was my competition. "Who are you?" The words hung in the air. He said, "I know you're young, but the key to opportunity is preparation." I hadn't dreamed of actually putting in that much work on my own without getting paid for it. That lesson has paid for that flight many times over. If it's what I want to do, am I doing it now? If no one is paying me, am I doing it anyway? I didn't really want to compose or I would have been composing. I wanted money for nothing. How often do we hear people say, "Give me the big job, then I'll work like someone with the big job." The truth is, people get the big job because they are already acting "as if" they had it.

From that point on, preparation became the name of the game. When I was out of work, I would hire myself. I pretended I needed to memorize and stage an opera and went to my own rehearsals. I learned things I didn't have to. When I was waiting at the bus stop, I was studying a new language or memorizing a song. When the opportunity came for me to do my first compact disc, someone approached me and offered to foot the five-figure bill, then added, "Can you start recording now?" I was ready. I had prepared for this moment. When tenors become ill (which they do all the time) and I am called in to replace them, I am ready. The operas are fresh. I work on them when I don't have to.

It is astonishing how many able-bodied people wait for a bus or sit on a train doing nothing to learn a new skill or make themselves more valuable. There are too many people in this society sitting around. Okay, you're out of work. Well, hire yourself! Spend the time learning a second language or picking up a new skill. It doesn't cost anything. Join the only 3% of Americans who possess a library card. There's so much available. Learn how to speak and communicate well. The secret of having more in life is not to expect that year by year you should get more from your boss, or hoping that the minimum wage will increase. It is to make yourself more valuable. The better you are, the more people will want you. There are actually those in this world who believe that they were forced into this world against

Don't Believe It!

their wills by their parents. As a result, they believe the world owes them a living. Life is a privilege and a joy. I believe that we chose to be here. Try that belief on for size and see how it changes your attitude.

The answers we seek to our problems are out there. The next time you have a problem, get out a piece of paper and number the paper from one to ten. Then write down ten solutions to your problem. Be creative. Don't evaluate or judge your solutions. Just write. You'll be surprised at what you come up with. This act will move your mind away from problem mode and into creative mode. The mere act of numbering your paper will tell your brain that you believe there are ten ways to deal with this. And there are! Your brain is amazing when you get out of the way and let it work. Keep your focus on the solutions and they will come.

Don't believe that:

1. focusing on problems brings happiness or answers.
2. you don't need to prepare for opportunities.
3. there are not at least ten answers to your problem.
4. your happiness depends on others.
5. you should reject help out of pride.
6. miracles don't happen.
7. if you have nothing to do, you can't create something to do.
8. you'll get more money without making yourself more valuable.
9. New York subways will always drop you off where you expect.

Chapter 18

The Inner Voice Hearer

*I believe in intuition and inspiration; at times I feel
certain I am right while not knowing the reason.*
— *Albert Einstein*

My goals have kept me very busy over the years. In fact, I was so focused that I really never tried to find time to develop any kind of deep relationships. I didn't plan on getting married until after college because I was just too occupied with other things. Then, at college, I met Melissa. We spent time together talking and sharing things and she quickly became my best friend. I had only known her a few months when something inside me said, "This is the one. You want to spend your life with her." I was shocked at this little voice inside me. I had no intention of getting involved romantically with anyone. I proposed. Interestingly enough, the same little voice told her to accept. Then, we went away to work for the summer— she to Iowa and I to California. At the end of the summer, as agreed, we met again the night before our wedding. We hardly knew each other. Logic seemed to dictate that I was making a really stupid decision. We looked into each other's eyes that night and were strangely calm. We both had an inner assurance that this was the right thing to do.

I know this all sounds cosmic, illogical, and somewhat religious. But I have a distinct memory of those feelings that transcended logic, that confirmed to my inner-self that we were making the right decision. I believe in this "inner-voice." I believe we all have access to it and that learning to hear it is a skill that can be acquired.

In the biographies of famous and successful people, there generally comes a time when they have sudden flashes of insight or feelings that tell them to make an illogical decision that changes their life for the better. Some people call it intuition. Some believe it is a connection to some universal consciousness. Some believe it is God, while others believe that the subconscious mind puts the pieces of a complicated puzzle together and sends our body a message. Whatever you are willing to accept, it is a true phenomenon. Learning to hear this voice will be a major influence on the success of your decisions. We are all living the result of the decisions we have made in the past. It's great to have a little help along the way with these choices so we don't spend time experiencing things we don't need to experience.

When my wife and I graduated, we didn't know where to go. I wanted to continue studying but also needed to find a place that would give me the best singing opportunities for my career. I began by studying and contemplating the main cities I could move to. Ultimately, the inner voice spoke and we felt peace about moving to San Jose, California. I had no idea why we felt we needed to go there, but within a couple of years, I knew.

To set the stage, I need to explain how opera systems work. Opera companies in the U.S. run on a "per opera" system where a singer signs a contract, goes to a city for a few weeks, sings an opera, gets a check, then goes home to try to find another job. It's a hard life and American singers find it hard to build up experience, let alone have any serious relationships.

Germany, however, uses a "fest" contract system. This means singers live in one city, sing the leads in the local opera house, get benefits, and go home to their families in the evening. As a result, many American singers go to Europe to live. I gave you this little history because when I moved to San Jose, I had no idea that in two years that Opera San José would be the first to start a "fest" style opera company in the United States. Nor did I know that I would be the first tenor in the U.S. to be offered one of these contracts. Suddenly, I was the house tenor, singing all the leads, with benefits, 'perqs', and an ability to go home to my wife every evening. As the company received national attention, I received more exposure in a short period of time than any young American singer I knew.

Don't Believe It!

Hearing and trusting that voice can be tricky at first. In fact it can by tricky throughout your life. The voice is subtle. When your mind and body are at peace, it is most perceptible. When you are depressed or angry it is difficult to hear. It is also impeded by mind- and body-altering substances. When your body is screaming and loaded with chemicals, how can you expect to hear anything? This is why so many people meditate, pray, or fast. Reaching deeper levels of consciousness or getting in touch with the quiet places of peace within us is a foundation of most of the great religions of the world. Being able to receive answers through such practices is attested to by too many in the world to be ignored.

Although many have those experiences, and many are trying to improve upon their experience to quiet the mind, no one is perfect. Some hear more than others, and others go through dry spells.

When I left San Jose, it was because of one of these clear inner signals. I knew when I was supposed to leave, and where I was supposed to go. But after I moved, I had one of these dry spells. I was terribly impatient. I wanted some kind of miracle to manifest itself right away. It did not. Impatience can be the worst killer of the inner voice. I have come to believe that things happen when they are supposed to happen. Pushing some things only makes them worse. This was a hard lesson for me to learn considering the aggressive way I have always pursued by desires. You know I hate to wait in lines. My impatience finally led me to abandon the voice I had previously heard and try to force the issue. I decided that where I was living wasn't logical but that I would have a better life in Germany. I got on a plane and went. I began to audition for jobs. Then, shortly after I had begun, I was standing in a

The Inner Voice Hearer

train station and looking around, when suddenly, I had an eerie experience. It seemed as if I were watching a movie of myself from a distance and I knew I was in the wrong picture. This wasn't my movie! It's hard to explain, but I knew I needed to go back right away. As a result of that decision, I was in the right place to have the opportunity to make my San Francisco debut, meet the sponsor of my first compact disc and have the child we were unable to have for eleven years. The chain of events continues to this very day and regularly astounds me.

I believe you need to know this information if you want to understand the full nature of the Risk Taker. You don't have to spend your life fighting the Dream Killers. In fact, you don't need to fight at all. Simply don't believe them. Risk Takers don't fight the current, they make their own rivers. They don't believe that:

1. there's no such thing as intuition.
2. all the best decisions are logical.
3. you can't learn to hear that inner voice, feel those promptings, or see in the minds eye where you need to be.
4. you can't trust your feelings.
5. you have to have a reason before you do what you know is right.
6. if you don't know what to do, you should go to Germany.

Chapter 19

The Everybody Lover

Love your enemies, bless them that curse you, do good to them that hate you, and pray for them which despitefully use you, and persecute you....For if ye love them which love you, what reward have ye?
-Matt. 5:44,46

I have the cure for stage fright! Earlier I told you to learn to be willing to fall on your face despite your fears. Well, guess what. That's only the first step. You don't have to fear at all. It took me a long time to figure out the answer and I fell on my face many times before I discovered it.

My first professional opera was a case in point. I

Don't Believe It!

was scared to death. I was stiff as a board and walked like a little stick man on stage.

The leading lady I was with was just the opposite. She seemed at home on the stage. She seemed to drink the experience in. Why wasn't she afraid? I watched her very carefully. To add to the nervousness, I was supposed to sing a high C at the end of my aria and then kiss her. It was my first kiss on stage. I was a wreck. During a dress rehearsal, I sang my aria and hit the high C at the end. Instead of getting ready to kiss me, the leading lady gave a short scream and jumped back away from me in fear. Oh no, I thought, I must have bad breath or something. Instead I found out that I had a nervous tick of rolling my eyes back in my head whenever I went for a high note. My eyes are fairly large to begin with, so when I did this, I looked like some kind of zombie from a sci-fi movie. It wasn't really conducive to the romantic mood, to be sure. I was so self-conscious that I didn't perform again for a year.

Why was I afraid?! I didn't stop searching. After talking to many people and reading many books, one answer began to emerge above the rest. Here it is: Love and fear cannot exist in your heart at the same time. If you fear in some situations, you simply haven't learned how to love in those same instances.

But it can be so hard! How do you love people during an audition who are only there to judge you? How do you love critics you know are in the audience? How do you love an audience that you believe hates you? If 90% of my audience likes my performance, I feel lucky. Anytime you present or sell a product or idea to masses of people, some people just won't like it. Or, perhaps, they will just not like you. The mere thought that anyone is in the audience with ill will towards them will freeze up some of the most talented people. That's because talent, ability, or skill have nothing to do with love. There are so many stories of talented performers who are scared to death back stage and literally have to be pushed on to perform. Once on stage, the love sometimes kicks in and they realize they are not going to die. The best performers know they have a gift to give and give it freely. If some don't appreciate or accept the gift, they offer it anyway. "Here is my gift," they inwardly say, "here is my most private self I give to you freely for your judgment or pleasure."

    Getting to the point of loving your enemies is not an easy thing. Expectations play a large role as well. When you are an audience member, the amount of love you show toward fellow performers will usually be the same amount you will expect when you are on stage. What you expect while on stage usually comes true as well. If you expect them to hate you, they probably will. Expectations of love usually bring love back. Whom would you rather watch? Someone with superior skill but shows a disdain or fear of you while they perform? Or would you prefer someone of less ability that you know loves you completely and gives their gift freely without fear? I know my answer. It's hard to like someone who expects the worst of you. We as humans generally crave love more than talent or ability. Keep that in mind when you begin to pursue your dreams. When you start to spread your ideas, products, services, and skills to the masses, love will help you spread it further. But more important than that, it will bring you joy and happiness. You may have all of the material success in the world and yet be miserable because you never learned this single skill.

Don't Believe It!

Love is a risky thing. You open yourself to potential pain. Some people try love once or twice in their lives and the experience is so painful that they shut down in order to protect themselves emotionally. They vow never to love again. Unfortunately, these people are not alive. This risk is always worth it. The potential joy far outweighs the possible pain from rejection. As humans, we were born to feel and experience both joy and pain. We are here to discover the opposition of all things. Without your awareness of rejection, you wouldn't appreciate the joy of acceptance. Without the bitter, the sweet would be tasteless.

Now you have an answer to many kinds of fear. However, it's one thing to read about it and quite another for you to get on the stage of life and experience it without any safety nets. If this book has been about anything, it's been about learning not to fear what others may say or do to destroy your dreams. Love is the only way to dispel this fear forever.

So, remember not to believe that:

1. you can't overcome your fear of others.
2. everyone will love you or what you do.
3. you should only love those who love you first.
4. love and fear can exist in your heart at the same time.
5. the risk of love isn't worth it.
6. you should emotionally protect yourself from rejection.
7. you can't be happy unless you're loved and accepted by everyone.
8. rolling your eyes back in your head will improve your high notes.

Chapter 20

The Faith Spreader

The music teacher came twice each week to bridge the awful gap between Dorothy and Chopin.
-George Ade

After all the nasty things I've said about our educational systems, let me tell you about two teachers who did it the right way and positively affected my life. These two teachers were an exception in my life because they went out of their way to encourage and uplift when the facts were against them.

The first was my high school orchestra teacher Mildred Cole. When I wasn't a terrific piano player, she believed in my potential. She gave me challenging tasks far above my capabilities and believed I could

Don't Believe It!

figure out how to get to a new level. When I wasn't taking piano lessons, she helped me find a way to take them. She gave me opportunities to perform and use my abilities all over the community. She taught me to love classical music. She entered me in festivals and stayed after school with me to practice. When I composed a piece, she played it at the spring concert herself. When I wrote a piece for the orchestra, she let me conduct it. She believed in my abilities when few did. She went the extra mile literally hundreds of times, encouraging me to believe in myself.

She was a Faith Spreader. I never heard her discourage a single student regardless of their abilities. She had learned that part of the quest we all have for happiness is fulfilled when we share what we have with others. When we spend our lives getting and never giving, we are sorry people indeed. The funny thing is, the more love you give away, the more comes right back to you. The last rule of the Risk Taker is to help others to believe.

After the two university professors had told me that I could not sing, I followed their advice. I half believed them. I went through many majors at the university. But I was never satisfied. Then one day, a graduate student and part time teacher, Becky Wilcox (now Wilberg), came to me and said, "You know, I bet you could sing if given half a chance. I want you to come to my office for a couple of free voice lessons." I went. She taught me an Italian song then she said, "Now I think you should sing for some of the voice faculty." I didn't realize that I was auditioning for a voice scholarship against about 130 other singers. I got it. I was floored.

Becky not only believed in me when others wouldn't, but she also put her time on the line to back up what she said. And her time was valuable. She was more than a normal graduate student. She loved to learn. She always had multiple majors and seemed to care less about the degree than the knowledge she was gaining. One day I was sharing a strong opinion I had with her. I had a habit of being very opinionated about things. Abruptly, she disagreed with me. She began quoting texts and treatises I had never even heard of. After about ten minutes, I had changed my strong opinion. Then with a twinkle in her eye, she told me that she was testing me. Then she revealed that she shared my original opinion. I felt like an idiot, but she taught me an important thing. That no matter how smart you get, someone always has a differing opinion. I learned a lot about the value of opinions—especially my own.

Yet regardless of how intelligent Becky was (which was very), she didn't use it to persuade others to give up their dreams. She certainly had the intellectual power to do just that. Instead she used her time and talents to build others up even when there was no evidence that they could succeed.

As you pursue your dreams, you can bet that there is someone more intelligent than you who will think you are wasting your time. But there will also be someone of equal brilliance who believes in you. Which one should you believe then? You may not even be smart enough to understand either side of the argument for and against your dreams.

If you make a mistake by going for that lofty goal, you will learn and grow much more than if you didn't have a dream at all. Whether you achieve the dream or not, you got something out of the process. It doesn't matter what your goal is. In fact what you achieve

Don't Believe It!

matters so much less than what you learn in the path. If you become a concert pianist, great! But that is less important than who you will become along the journey.

I didn't know this when I gave my first piano recital at age eighteen. I practiced four hours a day for a year. In an hour the concert was over. I wondered if that was all there was. What a letdown. I hadn't yet realized that the joy of life is found in the journey, and not the destination.

Too much of society has turned toward instant gratification. They no longer see the road of responsibility or the pathways of personal growth. Some get so confused with intelligent disagreement that they head apathetically down alleyways, deciding not to believe anything. They fear judgment, so they stay in their circles of safety. But we were not born to be safe! We were born to believe in something. We were born to turn those beliefs into actions. We were born to risk convention. We were born to fall on our faces with the world watching. We were born to get up with a smile on our faces after this happens.

If you're going to err, err on the side of your dream. Err loudly. Be wrong at the top of your voice. Believe something. Above all, believe that:

1. you were born to accomplish wonderful things.
2. your dreams are worth striving for.
3. you deserve your dreams.
4. the risks are worth it.
5. you are unique and exceptional.
6. when you appear on stage at Lincoln Center, you are not in the Twilight Zone...

So sing!

For books, newsletters, seminars, and other calendar events featuring Dan Montez visit:

www.danmontez.com